Play, PROJECTS, and Preschool Standards

*This book is dedicated to the young children of the world,
with the fervent wish that they might all experience and retain a
Sense of Wonder AND Joy in Learning.*

Play, Projects, and Preschool Standards

Nurturing Children's Sense of Wonder and Joy in Learning

Gera Jacobs

Kathy Crowley

Foreword by Marilou Hyson

CORWIN PRESS
A SAGE Publications Company
Thousand Oaks, CA 91320

For information:

Corwin Press
A Sage Publications Company
2455 Teller Road
Thousand Oaks, California 91320
www.corwinpress.com

Sage Publications Ltd.
1 Oliver's Yard
55 City Road
London, EC1Y 1SP
United Kingdom

Sage Publications India Pvt. Ltd.
B-42 Panchsheel Enclave
Post Box 4109
New Delhi 110 017   India

Printed in the United States of America

Library of Congress Cataloging-in-Publication Data

Jacobs, Gera.
Play, projects, and preschool standards: Nurturing children's sense of wonder and joy in learning/Gera Jacobs and Kathy Crowley.
       p. cm.
Includes bibliographical references and index.
ISBN 1-4129-2801-X or 978-1-4129-2801-4 (cloth: alk. paper)
ISBN 1-4129-2802-8 or 978-1-4129-2802-1 (pbk.: alk. paper)
   1. Early childhood education—Activity programs. 2. Creative activities and seat work.
   3. Play. I. Crowley, Kathy. II. Title.

LB1139.35.A37J36 2007
372.21—dc22   2006020222

This book is printed on acid-free paper.

07   08   09   10   10   9   8   7   6   5   4   3

Acquisitions Editor:	Stacy Wagner
Editorial Assistant:	Joanna Coelho
Production Editor:	Beth A. Bernstein
Copy Editor:	Carla Freeman
Typesetter:	C&M Digitals (P) Ltd.
Proofreader:	Anne Rogers
Indexer:	Judy Hunt
Cover Designer:	Monique Hahn
Graphic Artist:	Lisa Riley

Contents

Foreword   ix
Marilou Hyson

Preface   xi

Acknowledgments   xiii

About the Authors   xv

1. Addressing Preschool Standards in
   Developmentally Appropriate Ways   1
   - Defining the Standards   1
   - Meeting the Needs of All Children   3
   - Addressing Standards Through Engaging Experiences and Activities   3
   - Assessing Progress Toward Meeting the Standards   9
   - Summary   10

2. Designing the Environment With the Child in Mind   13
   - Creating a Welcoming Environment   13
   - Building Relationships   13
   - The Power of Choice   16
   - Arranging the Room for Exploration and Learning   18
   - Materials for Creating Engaging Interest Areas   18
   - Scheduling the Day for Play and Learning   21
   - Summary   22

3. Developing Positive Approaches to Learning and
   Social-Emotional Development   25
   *Developing Curiosity and Eagerness; Initiative and Persistence; Problem
   Solving and Reflection; Invention and Imagination; Self-Concept and
   Self-Confidence; Regulating Emotions; Respect and Appreciation of
   Similarities and Differences; and Pro-Social Behaviors and Cooperation*
   - Sample Early Learning Guidelines for Approaches to Learning   26
   - Sample Early Learning Guidelines for Social-Emotional Development   27
   - Developing Positive Approaches to Learning and Social-Emotional
     Development Through Projects   27
   - Designing the Environment   28
   - Addressing Standards Through Engaging
     Experiences and Activities   29

Supporting Children Who Are Bilingual Learners   37
Working With Children's Individual Needs   38
Summary   39

4. **Exploring the World Through Science**   41
Science as Inquiry; Physical Science; Life Science; Earth and Space Science;
Science and Technology; Science, Environment, and Society
    Sample Early Learning Guidelines for Science   42
    Exploring the World and Science Through Projects   43
    Designing the Environment   43
    Addressing Standards Through Engaging Experiences and Activities   44
    Supporting Children Who Are Bilingual Learners   54
    Working With Children's Individual Needs   55
    Summary   55

5. **Learning About Our Community Through Social Studies**   57
Families/Cultures; Community/Civics; History/Time;
Geography/Places, People, and Environments; and Economics
    Sample Early Learning Guidelines for Social Studies   58
    Learning About Our Community and Social Studies Through Projects   58
    Designing the Environment   59
    Addressing Standards Through Engaging Experiences and Activities   60
    Supporting Children Who Are Bilingual Learners   66
    Working With Children's Individual Needs   66
    Summary   67

6. **Engaging Children in Meaningful Literacy**   69
Reading; Writing; Listening and Phonological Awareness; Speaking/
Communicating and Oral Language Development; and Learning New Languages
    Sample Early Learning Guidelines for Language and Literacy   70
    Engaging Children in Meaningful Literacy Through Projects   70
    Designing the Environment   71
    Addressing Standards Through Engaging Experiences and Activities   73
    Supporting Children Who Are Bilingual Learners   85
    Working With Children's Individual Needs   86
    Summary   87

7. **Making Mathematics Inviting**   89
Number Sense and Operations; Shapes/Geometry; Measurement;
Data Analysis and Probability; and Patterns/Algebra
    Sample Early Learning Guidelines for Mathematics   90
    Making Mathematics Meaningful Through Projects   91
    Designing the Environment   92
    Addressing Standards Through Engaging Experiences and Activities   92
    Supporting Children Who Are Bilingual Learners   98
    Working With Children's Individual Needs   99
    Summary   99

8. **Fostering Creativity Through the Arts**   101

Visual Arts; Music; Creative Movement; and Dramatic Play

   Sample Early Learning Guidelines for Creative Arts   102
   Fostering Creativity in the Arts Through Projects   103
   Designing the Environment   104
   Addressing Standards Through Engaging Experiences and Activities   105
   Supporting Children Who Are Bilingual Learners   113
   Working With Children's Individual Needs   113
   Summary   114

9. **Promoting Physical Development and Healthy Lifestyles**   117

Gross Motor; Fine Motor; and Health and Safety

   Sample Early Learning Guidelines for Physical Development and Health   118
   Promoting Physical Development and Healthy Lifestyles Through Projects   119
   Designing the Environment   119
   Addressing Standards Through Engaging Experiences and Activities   122
   Supporting Children Who Are Bilingual Learners   127
   Working With Children's Individual Needs   128
   Summary   129

10. **Putting It All Together**   131

   Addressing Standards in Developmentally Appropriate Ways   131
   Addressing Standards and Benchmarks Through
      Projects, Studies, and Themes   132
   Supporting the Transition to Kindergarten   136
   Final Thoughts   137

Resources   139

   Signs for Interest Areas   139
   Assessing Children's Progress Toward Standards   144
   Sample Group Observation Tool for Language and Literacy   145
   Sample Individual Child Observation Tool for Language and Literacy   147
   Children's Books and Music   148
   Resources for Teaching Bilingual Learners   150
   Assessment Materials   151
   Helpful Web Sites   151

References   153

   For Further Reading   155

Index   157

Foreword

Early childhood educators have young children's best interests at heart. For this reason, teachers today are often challenged by and worried about the expectations in states' early learning standards. Teachers ask many questions: How can I apply what is in these lists of what children should know and be able to do? Are such standards really appropriate for very young children? Do they fit with my beliefs about the value of exploration and play? Do I have to stop what I've been doing? Are we in danger of turning children away from the joy of learning? And what about the increasing number of children in my class who are second-language learners or have significant disabilities and developmental delays?

In *Play, Projects, and Preschool Standards*, Gera Jacobs and Kathy Crowley have written an informative, friendly book to help teachers who are asking these kinds of questions. Its recommendations are consistent with current thinking about the value of standards and about what is needed to implement early learning standards effectively. The authors have been leaders in developing their own state's early learning standards. Although every set of standards is different, readers in any state can readily apply the principles and suggestions found in this book.

For example, a focus on the "whole child" is a central principle in the early childhood profession. While providing valuable ideas for addressing standards in the "academic" areas, the authors give equal attention to children's development and learning in areas such as social and emotional competence, physical development, and positive approaches to learning. Again, this emphasis is in line with research about the essential foundations of young children's success.

Both authors also have extensive practical experience with using projects and themes to organize the early childhood curriculum. With many examples, they show how children's interests can spark extended explorations of important topics. With teacher guidance and support, these explorations can lead to progress in relation to multiple early learning standards and benchmarks. Although this is not the only approach to curriculum planning, it is familiar to many teachers, allows rich opportunities for in-depth study, and naturally promotes integration across content areas as well as differentiation for children with varied background experiences, abilities, and disabilities.

Several specific features of this book make it especially useful to practitioners and to those who may be preparing to work with young children and their families. The book starts with the basics: Before discussing specific content areas—literacy, mathematics, social studies, and so on—and the standards and learning approaches for each area, Jacobs and Crowley begin with general suggestions about creating environments, relationships, and experiences to support all children's development. As I read these pages and those that followed, I saw images of welcoming, playful preschool programs, in which joy and just plain fun are not the opposite of learning.

Another helpful aspect of the book is that the authors, one of whom is currently a kindergarten teacher, give detailed suggestions for activities, projects, and experiences that will help support children's progress in relation to standards. These are not scripts or recipes, but they are specific enough for even inexperienced teachers. And for experienced teachers, the ideas in this book will seem familiar and nonthreatening—yes, they can indeed use what they already know and what their children love, but they can also enhance and expand their favorite activities, enriching the educational benefits of everyday experiences.

Also valuable is the book's treatment of diversity. Instead of having a separate chapter about disabilities and about culture and language, every chapter includes specific suggestions for making the standards and related activities meaningful to diverse children and families. In this way, the authors model a truly inclusive approach, encouraging teachers to think of children's common needs and interests, while accommodating individual characteristics.

This book will do much to answer the questions of the challenged and worried teacher and, more important, will motivate teachers to construct their own understanding and implementation of preschool standards. The suggestions and resources in *Play, Projects, and Preschool Standards* will help both new and experienced teachers to build their confidence and take some new, exciting steps. As they see children's positive responses to the engaging environments and experiences created with the help of this book, teachers will be encouraged to explore and renew their commitment to all children and families.

—Marilou Hyson, PhD
Senior Consultant, National Association for the Education of Young Children
Affiliate Faculty, Applied Developmental Psychology, George Mason University

Preface

One evening, my twin daughters, Katie and Bridget, were sitting around the kitchen table, studying for the next day's social studies test on "Communities" in their primary-grade classroom. They took turns responding as I asked questions. Katie felt especially well prepared because her teacher had loaned her the teacher's guide, since there weren't enough books for all the students in the class. When I asked the final question from the book, "What do communities use school buildings for in the evening when school is over?" Katie beamed and jumped out of her chair: "I know that one—I remember— *Answers may vary!*" Bridget looked at her quizzically and said, "Uh, uh, no—that's not right."

It took me a moment to realize what had happened. I sat in disbelief as I realized that my daughter had memorized exactly what the teacher's guide had written under this question: "Answers may vary." There wasn't just one right answer, there could be several correct answers. I asked Katie if she knew what her answer meant. Katie was obviously disappointed in my response; her face fell. She had known the answer word-for-word, but that didn't seem good enough. It was one of those peak moments for me in my teaching (and parenting) career, and I vowed to try to make sure that my students would understand what they were learning and that it would have meaning for them.

—Gera

Reflecting on that experience, we decided that if we ever wrote a book, *Answers May Vary* should be the title. As we started this book, we agreed that *Answers May Vary* wouldn't be the best title for this work, but that our goal for this book would be to share ideas that would capture children's imaginations, help them become engaged in their learning, and truly understand concepts.

A New Era in Education

Today, we are facing a new era in education. Standards have become a way of life in the educational world. When we first saw some of the kindergarten-through-12th-grade standards the children were expected to learn, we were concerned that some of the expectations for children in the younger grades did not seem to be developmentally appropriate. When we attended national conferences and heard them talk about having standards in preschool, our first reaction was negative. We didn't want the inappropriate standards we were seeing passed down to preschool. We listened as the discussion at national conferences and in the professional journals seemed to progress from "Should we have standards in preschool?" to "How do we make sure that our preschool standards are high quality and developmentally and culturally appropriate?"

When our state began working on its preschool standards, we were asked to help lead the effort. Although it seemed to be one more thing to add to a long list we already were having trouble keeping up with, we agreed. We knew we would have little room to complain if we hadn't done our part. We also knew we could have an influence in making sure that the standards were appropriate for preschool children and could lead to meaningful learning. As we wrote the standards, we were committed to making sure that those who read them would get the message that children from age 3 to 5 learn best through play and hands-on activities. This book will share that same message.

The Aim and Organization of This Book

The book is designed to provide support for preschool and prekindergarten teachers, early childhood special educators, child care providers, parents, and all who work with preschool-aged children, as well as those preparing to teach young children. Throughout the book, we occasionally use the words *classroom* or *room*, but we use these terms to refer to any place where children from age 3 to 5 learn and grow. Our work is based on the research in the field and documents from national organizations, including the following: National Association for the Education of Young Children; National Association of Early Childhood Specialists in State Departments of Education; International Reading Association; National Council of Teachers of English; National Council of Teachers of Mathematics; National Science Education Association; National Council for the Social Studies; National Association for Sport and Physical Education; and Consortium of National Arts Education Associations.

Chapter 1 provides an overview of preschool standards and how they can be met in developmentally appropriate ways through engaging, hands-on activities. Chapter 2 discusses the importance of relationships and describes how to set up the environment with engaging interest areas that will help children meet the standards. Chapters 3 through 9 present ideas on how to help children reach standards in each major curriculum area. These chapters contain suggestions for designing the environment; implementing engaging projects, experiences, and activities; supporting bilingual learners; and working with children's individual needs. These activities are designed for children from 3 to 5 years of age. Curriculum areas are discussed separately to correspond with preschool standards, but, in practice, these areas are all interrelated. The final chapter ties the information together, provides ideas for sample projects that will help children reach preschool standards, and offers suggestions to support children's transition to kindergarten. Information about children's books and songs, as well as other references mentioned throughout the chapters, are included in the Resources section at the end of the book.

Throughout the chapters, we have included samples of standards. These standards are actual preschool standards for South Dakota. Most states' standards may be found at each State Department of Education Web site and the National Childcare Information Center Web site. Although standards vary somewhat from state to state, the ideas and suggestions provided in this book can help all children progress toward meeting standards and building a strong foundation for a lifetime of learning.

Acknowledgments

W e would like to thank the South Dakota Early Learning Guidelines Panel for their work in creating the South Dakota Early Learning Guidelines; Betsy Pollock, Deb Barnett, and Rick Melmer at the South Dakota Department of Education; and Pat Monson and Carroll Forsch at the South Dakota Division of Child Care Services. We wish to express deep gratitude to Marcy Martin, Diane Lowery, Linda Reetz, Julie Olsen Edwards, Steve Miles, Angie Haas, Holly Mueller, Cheryl Schaeffer, Lora Trudeau, Amanda Mitchell and Liz Koerner for their review and comments on our manuscript, Teresa Piper for assistance with Spanish translation, and to Pam Kringle, children's librarian, for her suggestions of quality children's books. We are indebted to Marilou Hyson, senior consultant to the National Association for the Education of Young Children (NAEYC), for her expertise, insight, and words of encouragement on both this manuscript and the South Dakota Early Learning Guidelines. We offer sincere appreciation to Stacy Wagner, our editor, who has supported us through every step of this journey, along with Carla Freeman, copy editor and Beth Bernstein, production editor, for their expertise and guidance. Special thanks to Jerry Jacobs, Meriah Jacobs Frost, Merle Eintracht, Junella Kost, Margo Logue, Jim Frost, Carrie Roerig, Carmen Stewart, Michelle Bierle, Cindy Gutzman, Lynne Bye, Melissa Myron, Jade Anthofer, and the staff, administration, children, and families at the University of South Dakota Head Start Program, Vermillion School District Early Childhood Program, St. Agnes School, University of South Dakota Vucurevich Child Care Center, and the Center for Children and Families for their assistance with photographs that add life to the words on these pages. Finally, we would like to convey our eternal gratitude to our families, who gave us their time, suggestions, and support, and cheered us on. They believed in us, understood the time required for this project, and put up with dirty dishes, TV dinners, and many late nights. To all of you, we are deeply thankful!

Corwin Press gratefully acknowledges the contributions of the following reviewers:

Patricia A. Barto
Executive Director of Early Childhood
Cleveland Municipal School District
Cleveland, OH

Suzanne Beane
Prekindergarten teacher of students with special needs
Cypress Elementary School
New Port Richey, FL

Susan W. Cress
Associate Professor of Early Childhood and Elementary Education
Indiana University
South Bend, IN

Julie Olsen Edwards
NAEYC Governing Board Member, 2003-2007
Early Childhood Education Instructor
Cabrillo Community College
Aptos, CA

Sarah Farrell
Bilingual teacher
Colinas Del Norte Elementary School
Rio Rancho, NM

Karen Jurgensen
Title I teacher
Flour Bluff Primary School
Corpus Christi, TX

Marta Plata
Early Childhood Specialist
Assistant Principal
Rufino Mendoza Elementary School
Fort Worth, TX

Rosemarie Young
Past President, National Association for Elementary School Principals
Louisville, KY

About the Authors

Gera Jacobs is a professor of early childhood education at the University of South Dakota and taught preschool, kindergarten, and the elementary grades for many years. She has published articles in a number of national and regional journals and produced a CD-ROM on inclusion for young children with special needs. She has presented at numerous state, regional, and national conferences and has conducted many inservice presentations for teachers. She is a member of the National Association for the Education of Young Children (NAEYC) Governing Board and served on the NAEYC Affiliate Council. The Carnegie Corporation named her South Dakota Professor of the Year in 2002. She was chairperson of the South Dakota Early Learning Guidelines Panel, responsible for writing the preschool standards for South Dakota. Gera is now helping with South Dakota's efforts to establish public preschool.

Kathy Crowley is a kindergarten teacher and has taught preschool, kindergarten, and the elementary grades for many years. She provided child care in her home while her children were young and was director of an afterschool program. She is a member of several professional organizations and has presented at numerous state and regional conferences. Kathy served as vice president of the South Dakota Association for the Education of Young Children (SDAEYC), cochaired their state conference, and received the SDAEYC state service award in 2006. She was a member of the South Dakota Early Learning Guidelines Panel and is serving on the state committee to establish public preschool.

Addressing Preschool Standards in Developmentally Appropriate Ways

The early years of life form the foundation for all later learning and development. Rich experiences with engaging materials and caring adults during the preschool years lay the foundation for children to develop a lifelong love of learning and a positive sense of self-worth. Research has confirmed that experiences children have during the first years of life help to form vital connections in the brain that establish the framework for future learning. As children play, investigate their world, and participate in language-rich environments with supportive adults, they build these connections and grow in all areas of development.

Teachers, caregivers, and parents often wonder how best to help their children, what kinds of skills they should be learning, and how they can assist their children in attaining these skills. Preschool content standards provide direction by outlining goals most children can achieve during these early years.

Defining the Standards

Preschool content standards describe appropriate skills, knowledge, and understanding children can attain with support by the time they have finished their preschool years. There are different terms used to describe standards, but generally accepted definitions are provided below.

Standards are general statements that represent the information and/or skills that children should know and be able to do. Each standard area contains benchmarks that are subcomponents of standards that describe more concretely what children should know and be able to do at specific developmental levels (Bodrova, Leong, Paynter, & Semenov, 2000). For example, a standard for the Social/Emotional Area might be "Children demonstrate a positive self-concept and self-confidence in play and everyday tasks." A more specific benchmark under that standard could be "Children adjust to new situations."

In this book, the benchmarks that are provided describe children's performance at the end of their preschool years.

Each state has created its own unique preschool standards and refers to them by various names, including the following:

- Early Learning Guidelines
- Early Learning Standards
- Indicators
- Desired Results
- Early Learning and Development Benchmarks
- Preschool Teaching and Learning Expectations

Target ages for the standards vary somewhat, but they are generally designed for children 3 to 5 years of age. Ideally, preschool teachers, family home- and center-based child care providers, Head Start staff, administrators, early childhood special educators, parents, and all who work with preschool-aged children can use these standards.

The federal initiative Good Start, Grow Smart (2002) asked states to develop voluntary early learning guidelines in the areas of language and literacy, as well as mathematics that align with the state standards for kindergarten. This alignment ensures a continuum of learning experiences from preschool to kindergarten and the elementary grades. States have included other curricular areas as well to address the needs of the whole child. These early learning guidelines are available from the Department of Education in most states, as well as on the Internet, including the National Childcare Information Center Web site at http://www.nccic.org/pubs/goodstart/elgwebsites.html.

Preschool standards can guide our work with children and outline what most children will be able to know and do by the end of their preschool years. However, they should not be used as a means of keeping children from entering kindergarten. As educators, our emphasis should be on helping children achieve success in preschool and kindergarten; preschool standards can help us to do that. They describe skills and understandings that children can develop in a supportive environment during their preschool years that will help them start kindergarten ready to succeed. Three-year-old children are just beginning to make progress toward reaching most of the benchmarks. With the guidance of caring adults, they will continue to make progress throughout their preschool years.

Meeting the Needs of All Children

Although skills outlined in preschool standards are written to be achievable for most children by the end of their preschool years, each child is unique. Children develop at individual rates and have individual needs and characteristics. Within a group of typically developing children, there will be significant differences in their rates of development. Our goal should be that all children have opportunities to achieve their full potential, even though some of them won't reach all of the standards.

Children also come to us speaking a variety of languages. We can support children by encouraging the use of their first language while introducing the new language. The child's first language serves as the foundation for the acquisition of other languages. Throughout this book we will use the term *bilingual learners* to refer to children who are learning English as a new language, as well as children who know English and are learning their families' native languages. This term is also used to emphasize the importance of children retaining their home language as they learn the new language. More discussion on helping children learn a new language can be found in Chapter 6 and at the end of Chapters 3 through 9.

Addressing Standards Through Engaging Experiences and Activities

Designing curriculum is an ongoing process that involves understanding our children and their needs. Curriculum can be defined as "the content (knowledge, skills, and dispositions) to be taught and the plans for experiences through which learning will take place" (Copple & Bredekamp, 2006, p. 59). Early learning guidelines outline the content preschool children can learn.

Our challenge is making certain we are helping children reach these guidelines in developmentally appropriate ways.

What Research and the Experts Tell Us

Developmentally Appropriate Practice

"Developmentally Appropriate Practice (DAP) means teaching young children in ways that meet children where they are, as individuals and as a group; and helping each child reach challenging and achievable goals that contribute to his or her ongoing development and learning" (Copple & Bredekamp, 2006, p. 3). Adults make decisions about their work with children based on knowledge of child development (age appropriate), each individual child (individually appropriate), and the social and cultural contexts of the children (socially and culturally appropriate). DAP also requires that adults teach intentionally, purposefully planning curriculum and assessment with each child in mind. In developmentally appropriate programs, there is an awareness that children learn through relationships with responsive adults; active, hands-on involvement; meaningful experiences; and constructing their understandings of the world. Adults plan experiences and work side by side with children, helping them make sense of their world (Bredekamp & Copple, 1997; Copple & Bredekamp, 2006).

Learning and Play

Research has shown that children learn best through play. We need to encourage children to ask questions, explore, and discover through play and rich experiences with engaging materials. If we want children to truly learn and understand concepts, we should provide hands-on experiences that allow them to see how things work and help them to construct knowledge about the concepts:

- Children learn science concepts as they play at the water table and watch caterpillars turn into butterflies.
- They learn math as they build with blocks of various sizes and sort and classify toy dinosaurs.
- Literacy blossoms as children listen to stories and then retell the stories with puppets. It continues to grow as they sign their names to pictures they have drawn and make cards for their friends.
- Social skills develop as they play in the Dramatic Play Area, trying out adult roles, preparing pretend meals for each other, and learning to share materials.
- Motor skills develop as they run and play outside, ride tricycles, string beads, play with toy cars, and create with play dough.

What Research and the Experts Tell Us
Play

For many years, theorists have written about the importance of play for children's learning and development. Piaget (1952) believed that children learn best through play and their interactions with the environment. Bruner (1972) described play as the way children learn to solve problems that will later enable them to work through problems as an adult. According to Vygotsky, play "is the preeminent educational activity of early childhood" (Berk & Winsler, 1995, p. 57). Vygotsky (1978) believed play allows children to move forward in their development. "Play creates a zone of proximal development in the child. In play, the child always behaves beyond his average age, above his daily behavior; in play it is as though he was a head taller than himself" (p. 102). Brain research has also confirmed the importance of play and exploration to brain development (Shonkoff & Phillips, 2000; Shore, 1997).

The Project Approach

An effective way to help children learn is to use the Project Approach (Chard, 1998; Katz & Chard, 2000). In the Project Approach, children engage in an in-depth study of a topic. Adults observe children's interests, enthusiasm, and questions over time. After thoughtful discussions with the children, together they choose a project topic to investigate. The topic should be something worthy of an extended study and full of potential for children's exploration. There should also be enough materials, books, resource people, and possible field sites to visit. Another consideration before choosing a topic would be to ensure that standards could be met through the project, although most worthwhile topics will enable children to meet a whole host of standards. Children learn literacy, mathematics, science, social studies, the arts, social, emotional, and motor skills in the context of working on the project. The project could last for several weeks or longer, depending on the children's interest and resources available. The preschools in Reggio Emilia, Italy, which have been ranked as some of the best early childhood programs in the world, engage children in long-term projects (Edwards, Forman, & Gandini, 1998).

Phases of the Project Approach

Phase 1: Beginning the Project

Opening event, material, or story to spark additional interest

Brainstorming with the children possible areas to investigate in the project

Developing a web, including areas related to the topic that children wish to learn more about

Developing questions with the children that they would like to explore

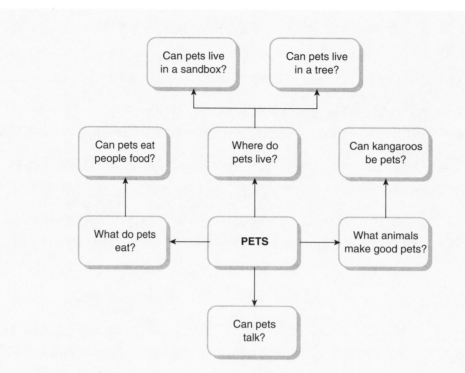

Phase 2: Investigation and Representation: Doing the Actual Work of the Project

Planning and participating in field visits

Inviting experts and visitors to share information on the topic

Reading, investigating, and gathering information

Playing in interest areas

Taking photographs

Drawing and dictating information they have learned

Documenting children's learning and progress

Phase 3: Concluding the Project

Completing documentation of the project

Culminating event to share the work of the project with others

Reflecting on what was learned through the project

Choosing a new topic or direction for the next project

A project might develop as you notice children talking about their pets. A conversation between Ella and James went something like this:

James: I have dogs.

Ella: I have two dogs, Kamey and Coco. Kamey is *so* black.

James: Um, I love to throw the tennis ball, and I love it when they win.

Ella: I play with them—give them kisses.

James: I love to feed them, and love it when they watch me paint with water.

You may also notice the children painting pictures of cats and dogs and choosing books related to pets in the Library Area. Children may be asking to bring their pets from home to show their friends and are especially interested in a neighborhood dog that wanders by each day. The following chart shows how you might proceed through the different phases of the project, depending on the children's interests. The plan would evolve as the project progresses, based on the children's questions, interests, and ideas.

A Project on Pets

Phase 1

- Introduce a real puppy and read a book, such as *Franklin Wants a Pet,* as an opening event.
- Make a topic web with the children by brainstorming all the possible topics that could be included in a project on pets.
- As children dictate, list on large chart paper what they already know about the topic as well as questions they would like to investigate.

Phase 2

- Invite parents to bring in family pets or pictures of their pets, and ask children to share how they care for them.
- Invite a veterinarian, parent, or someone knowledgeable about pets in to talk with the group, and plan a trip to a local pet store if this is an option.
- Take walks to observe animals and pets in the neighborhood, and encourage parents to walk with their children as well.
- Read books about pets to individuals and small groups. Add books to the Library Area and books on tape to the Listening Area that deal with pets.
- Set up the Dramatic Play Area as a veterinarian's office or a pet store, so children can further explore the new information they are learning.
- Introduce a new pet to the classroom, such as a fish or guinea pig. Have children investigate the kind of environment, food, and care the pet would need. Weigh and measure the pet weekly, and chart this information on a graph.
- Revisit the topic web and list of questions frequently.

- Provide materials for children to create imaginary pets from play dough, clay, and other creative art materials. Help them to name their pets and dictate stories about them.
- Encourage children to represent other information they have learned with additional drawings and creations.

Phase 3

Conclude the project with the children by helping them decide how to demonstrate and share what they have learned. This could include setting up a small pet store with their new creations and stories. Children could help make signs and invitations for parents to come in to listen to stories the children dictated and see all that they have accomplished.

Science and social studies themes have the potential of offering meaningful, interesting project topics for exploration. Looking over preschool standards and benchmarks in these areas may provide inspiration for quality topics to investigate. As children explore science and social studies ideas, they will not only learn the science and social studies concepts, but they will be learning in all other areas of the curriculum as well.

There are many effective ways to help children learn skills and concepts in addition to the Project Approach. It is important that adults working with preschool children be knowledgeable about standards and developmental milestones appropriate for their children. By keeping these in mind, they can intentionally plan activities and experiences that will address these standards and milestones.

Assessing Progress Toward Meeting the Standards

Documenting children's progress toward achieving standards and benchmarks should be done in ways that are developmentally appropriate for preschool-aged children (McAfee, Leong, & Bodrova, 2004). Assessing children helps us find each child's *zone of proximal development,* which Vygotsky (1978) believed is where all real learning occurs. This zone is the distance between what a child is capable of doing independently and what he or she can do with assistance (Bodrova & Leong, 1996). When we know what children can do on their own, we can use preschool standards to help us determine what additional skills we can work on to help them progress in their development.

Observing and Recording

Observation tools, checklists, and anecdotal records can help us determine the zone of proximal development for each child. You can make an observation tool by using a list of your state standards. This tool could be designed to keep track of the whole group by listing specific benchmarks down the side and the children's names across the top in a grid. This information can then be transferred to separate forms for individual children, to show their growth throughout the year. The Resources section at the back of this book contains sample observation tools that can be adapted, using your own state standards.

While observation tools and checklists are helpful, we should not assume that addressing a standard one time is sufficient. A single project or activity is not enough. We need to intentionally plan multiple opportunities for children to grow in their skill, knowledge, and understanding and assess their growth over time.

Observations and assessment of children should be made and recorded while children are engaged in play and daily activities. Children often demonstrate their growing understandings as they try out roles in the Dramatic Play Area, create artwork, build, and tell stories. Standardized paper-and-pencil tests are not appropriate assessment measures for preschool children.

Portfolios

Children's growth can also be documented through collections of their work in portfolios. These portfolios could include drawings, samples of children's writing and other work, photographs, and even audio and/or videotape recordings. Asking children to take part in choosing which pieces of their work to include in their portfolios to show their growth will help children think about what they have learned and help them be more aware of the learning process. Benchmarks addressed by items in the portfolio could be written on the back of the work samples.

Other Developmentally Appropriate Assessments

There are several developmentally appropriate, systematic assessment tools designed to help assess children's progress. These include the Creative Curriculum Developmental Continuum Assessment System, the Preschool Child Observation Record from High/Scope, and The Work Sampling System (see the "References and Further Reading" section for more information on these resources).

In the Project Approach, teachers often make documentation panels that document the work of the project over time. The panels can include children's drawing, writing, and photographs of the children at work (Helm, Beneke, & Steinheimer, 1998). Children's assessments and progress should be shared with families so they can support children's growth as well.

Summary

Early learning guidelines or preschool standards can help guide our work with children. They outline skills, knowledge, and understanding that most children can attain during their preschool years with the support of caring adults. Children learn these best through play and engaging hands-on activities. An effective way to help children reach early learning guidelines is through the Project Approach, which engages children in an in-depth study of a topic of interest. Assessing children's progress can inform our work with children by showing us what they are able to do and where they still need assistance. Assessment should be carried out in developmentally appropriate ways, while children are engaged in play, through observations, checklists, and documentation.

Designing the Environment With the Child in Mind

Creating an engaging, exciting place for children to play, learn, and grow is one of our major responsibilities. Maria Montessori has been credited with saying that the primary role of the teacher is to prepare the environment for children. What a wonderful job that is for us, to design a space that will motivate children to discover, explore, and develop!

Creating a Welcoming Environment

The environment we create communicates our beliefs about children, their importance, and how they learn. The environment should be friendly and homelike, helping children and families feel at ease from the moment they arrive. To create this welcoming environment, add photographs of the children and their families and artwork created by the children. All this can be at children's eye level so they can view it easily. Green plants, pretty tablecloths, flowers, and colorful fabrics at the window and throughout the room are just a few things that add to a warm, inviting setting. Comfortable furniture can be added, in which parents and children can relax, talk, and read a book together (Curtis & Carter, 2003).

Building Relationships

When children walk through the door into our programs, they need to feel that they are welcome, respected, and valued. Building a strong, caring relationship with each child is the best way to instill this sense of worth and belonging. Greeting children individually at the beginning of the day and letting them know how glad we are that they are able to

TRY THIS!

Take a look at your room from a child's perspective. What catches your interest and invites you to play? Are there things you could change or add that would enhance the environment for the children? Are there things you could do to create soft, cozy spaces where children could curl up with a good book or simply relax? Be on the lookout for colorful, shiny, textured, or natural objects and materials that children might find captivating or intriguing that you could add to your setting.

spend time with us is a wonderful way to build the relationship. Developing this relationship requires that we take time, listen, and have meaningful conversations with children throughout the day. According to Amy Baker and Lynn Manfredi/Petitt (2004),

> Children's early relationships teach them who they are and what they can expect from the world; their healthy brain development thrives on loving attachments and a secure sense of belonging. The best caregivers are those who are able to invest themselves emotionally and take children into their hearts. (p. 56)

Children who have secure relationships are more willing to tackle new challenges and are able to get more out of learning experiences.

Get to know your children as individuals; treasure them. While children are playing, building structures in the Block Area or creating in the Art Area, ask them to tell you about what they are doing. Show interest and let them know their efforts have worth. This will boost children's self-confidence and interest in learning.

In her book *Teaching in the Key of Life,* Mimi Brodsky Chenfeld (1993) urged those who work with children to spend time with children, believe in them, and teach from the heart:

> Talk with your children. Share and compare observations, questions, experiences, and wishes, wondering. Laugh together. . . . Our children need an environment sweetened with tender loving care, encouragement, inspiration, role models, and time—time to play, pretend, explore, experiment, and wonder; time to develop at their own pace and in their own special rhythms. When children learn in such safe, supportive settings under the gentle, constant guidance of loving adults, they prove over and over again that they are among the most creative members of this gifted and talented human family of ours. (p. 15)

Children will also feel more at ease, be willing to try, and learn more if they feel that they are valued members of the group. Children need to know that it is safe to take chances, confident that their attempts at learning will be accepted and supported. This can occur in an environment where children know that we respect them and there is mutual respect between the children. Developing a sense of community among the children will increase their motivation and decrease behavior concerns. This community spirit can grow by providing time for children to talk with each other, play with each other, sing with each other, and simply spend time with each other. Snacks and meals can be enjoyable times to talk and share together. End the day with a favorite big book, song, and shared excitement

about coming events. Each moment of the day offers opportunities for building relationships, discovery, play, learning, and joy!

Relationships With Families

When developing their accreditation criteria for early childhood programs, the National Association for the Education of Young Children (NAEYC, 2005) grounded its program standards in principles that stated, "Positive relationships between children and adults are fundamental to a harmonious environment that promotes learning and growth" (p. 8). In addition, their principles for high-quality programs embrace the idea that "families matter, both in terms of their influence on their own child or children and as partners with the program's administration and teaching staff working to maximize the quality of children's experiences" (p. 8). Building relationships with families is critical.

Children's learning potential can be dramatically increased when we form partnerships with their families. Let families know you consider them a vital part of the educational team working to help their children. Some tips for partnering with families include the following:

- *Sharing* information on the importance of spending quality time with their children, talking, listening, and enjoying a variety of experiences.
- *Encouraging* them to read to their children every day, making it an enjoyable, bonding time that includes rich conversations about favorite books, characters, and how the stories relate to their own lives.
- *Listening* to parents to find out more about children's interests and what works best for their children at home.
- *Providing* copies of your early learning guidelines or considering sending home one section of the guidelines each month, along with fun, hands-on ideas families can do together.

- *Explaining* that the guidelines can give parents information about the skills and knowledge most preschool age children are able to acquire by the end of their preschool years and that they will learn these best through play.
- *Informing* parents and guardians that they don't need to drill their children on academics. It is the relationship with their children that is of utmost importance and will help form a secure foundation that children can build on in the future.
- *Collaborating* with families to develop goals for children and solve any problems that may arise.

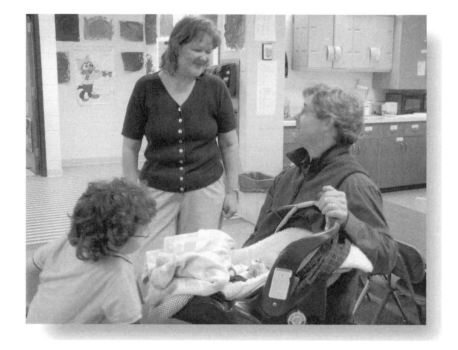

In the early childhood programs in Reggio Emilia, Italy, there is an underlying profound respect for each child and family that influences everything else that occurs. The entry area of the building is welcoming and designed so parents and guardians can visit, read posted information, and see panels of work the children have done in their project work. In Reggio, the image of the child as strong, capable, and full of potential is evident in the environment. Educators provide children with extended periods of time to explore and work on various aspects of a project, individually and in small groups. They set up the room so the children can continue to work on a piece of art or block construction over a period of several days, with the knowledge that they can return and further develop their work without feeling rushed (Wurm, 2005).

The Power of Choice

The room should be set up in a child-friendly fashion. Toys, blocks, and art supplies should be at the children's level, allowing them to have easy access to materials and grow in their independence. The room may include "interest areas," such as Blocks, Dramatic Play, Art,

Library, Sand and Water, Music, and Discovery/Science, where children can be actively engaged in their learning (Dodge, Colker, & Heroman, 2002). These areas can encompass all aspects of the curriculum, including literacy, math, science, and the arts. Children can become more deeply involved in the learning process at these areas. During the preschool years, the majority of time children are in the program should optimally be devoted to opportunities for them to choose which areas they wish to investigate. If there are special activities you want all children to benefit from, you can ask that everyone spend some time in that area during the day or by the end of the week. Children can learn concepts in a variety of subjects in any area of the room. As they build in the Block Area, they can be learning math, science, literacy, and social skills; this is true in the other interest areas as well.

Generally, children should be able to stay in an area as long as they are interested. This will allow them to become more deeply involved in an activity, as well as increase their attention spans. When we ask children to spend 10 or 15 minutes in a certain area and then switch to another area, we may be curbing their creativity, persistence, or ability to stay focused on a task. We also take away their ability to choose and opportunities to develop their independence. Some of the benefits of providing choice as children are involved in interest areas could include the following:

Consider setting up a special science activity with materials borrowed from a nearby museum, such as a collection of butterflies. Ask children to explore the materials by the end of the week before you return them.

- A decrease in behavior problems because children are more engaged and are encouraged to move around and be active, which is appropriate for their stage of development
- An increase in motivation and desire to learn, which in turn increases the amount of learning that takes place and the ability to retain that knowledge (Shalaway, 2005)
- More talking and idea sharing, increasing children's vocabularies, which is an essential requirement to becoming successful readers in the future (Neuman, Copple, & Bredekamp, 2000)

Interest areas give children many opportunities to practice the skills they are learning in more meaningful contexts, which leads to strengthening of these skills. While children are involved in interest areas, we have more time to work with individuals and small groups, allowing us to meet their individual needs and help them make progress in their learning and development.

In addition to established interest areas, use mats, towels, area rugs, or brightly colored fabrics to designate areas where children can be involved in activities. Materials for these activities can be stored in backpacks, lunchboxes, cloth bags, or plastic containers. Children can bring the materials to the mat or fabric and have a defined space for their play and work.

Arranging the Room for Exploration and Learning

It is important that the environment be arranged to promote learning and exploration.

What Research and the Experts Tell Us
The Importance of Active Learning and the Environment

Developmental research, theories of child development and learning (Piaget, 1952; Vygotsky, 1978), as well as findings from neuroscience suggest that we need to provide children with opportunities to be actively engaged in hands-on, meaningful learning. As children play and work with hands-on materials, they form connections in the brain. These connections, called *synapses,* become hardwired as permanent fixtures in the brain as they are used. They will form the foundation for later learning. A stress-free, engaging environment is optimal for the formation of these connections and children's learning. Too much stress, caused by unrealistic expectations and a variety of other stressors, can hamper the connections and children's development (Shore, 1997).

To arrange the room for hands-on activities in interest areas, we need to make use of available space, using all areas as opportunities for learning. This could include the following:

- Tables
- Walls
- Corners
- Available floor space

Materials for Creating Engaging Interest Areas

Reading Area

Variety of children's books

Children's magazines

Books on tape

Books made by children in the classroom

Comfortable places to sit and read

Writing Area

Variety of paper

Crayons, pencils, and washable markers

Rubber stamps and washable inkpads

Small chalkboards or whiteboards

Math Area

Natural objects, such as rocks, shells, and pinecones, for counting, measuring, sorting, graphing, and estimating

A variety of manipulatives—commercial and collected from home

Boxes of plastic cubes, milk jug lids, teddy bear counters, etc.

Rulers, meter sticks, tape measures, and other measuring devices

Calculators, abacus

Multicultural materials to count and measure, such as large, native beads

Discovery/Science Area

Magnifying glasses

Balance scales

Natural objects for observing, including rocks, shells, leaves, and pinecones

Classroom pets, butterfly gardens, tadpoles

Pulleys, gears, wheels, inclined planes

Magnets and trays with an assortment of materials to explore with the magnets

Dramatic Play Area

This area can begin as a Housekeeping Area with the following:

Dolls from a variety of cultures

Doll bed and doll clothes

Child-sized table and chairs

Toy refrigerator, stove, and sink

Dishes, pots, pans, and pretend food from a variety of cultures

Dress-up clothes

The Dramatic Play Area can be changed with projects and themes throughout the year, such as setting up a veterinarian's office during a project related to studying animals, using materials such as stuffed animals, a reception desk with paper and pencils for taking notes, and a children's doctor kit.

Computer Area

Software to go along with units, themes, and projects

Seating for two at each computer to promote social interaction

Water and Sand Area

Sand and water tables or large containers of sand and water

Measuring cups and spoons

Funnels

Strainers

Empty dishwashing soap bottles and hand soap dispenser pumps

Styrofoam, foil, and other materials to use for making boats

Sink-and-float materials

Toy animals

Art Area

Paper of various shapes, textures, and colors

Washable markers, crayons, and pencils

Multicultural markers, paints, crayons, and play dough

Watercolors, tempera, and fingerpaint

Materials for creativity, such as film containers, pieces of wood, glue, paint, and fabric

Printmaking items (potato mashers, other kitchen objects, sponges)

Collage materials

Smocks or paint shirts

Music and Movement Area

CD player or tape recorder

Headphones

A variety of children's music to listen to, including multicultural music

Musical instruments

Scarves

Interest areas can be labeled with the name of the area, as well as the standards that children are learning in the area. Samples of signs for interest areas can be found in the

Resources section at the back of this book. These can be enlarged or personalized to fit your own state's early learning guidelines.

Scheduling the Day for Play and Learning

Think of the entire day as an opportunity for children to learn through play. The way the day is scheduled has a great impact on how much children will learn and their attitudes toward learning. The beginning or "welcoming time" should be a time when we greet children individually and let them know we value and respect them. During this time, children can be hanging up coats; putting away books they borrowed; doing simple, inviting activities set out at tables; or looking at books in the Library Area. The remainder of the day should include time for large- and small-group activities, as well as time for children to choose activities in interest areas they would like to engage in alone or with others. A child could choose to start out playing in the Dramatic Play Area, preparing a pretend meal for friends and inviting others to join in when the meal is ready. Then, the child might choose to look at books in the Library Area for a while, retelling a story with puppets. From there, the child may decide to join others in building a block structure, and then enjoy playing at the water table at the end of the morning.

The schedule below could be used for an all-day program or adapted for a half-day preschool. Times can be changed to fit with your schedule. The schedule should be flexible to meet the needs and interests of the children. Any of the activities can be done either outside or inside, depending on your setting and climate. Children love spending time outdoors, and many activities become more motivating and interesting outside.

These times should be flexible and allow children maximum time for hands-on exploration and learning. Snacks can also be served in buffet style, either indoors or outdoors, to allow for more uninterrupted time for play and discovery. Time for children to play and investigate in the interest areas and work on project-related activities could be extended to last throughout the majority of the morning and afternoon without breaking up the schedule.

Sample Daily Schedule

8:00	Welcoming time (greet children and invite them to play with activities set out on tables, look at books, talk with each other, and say good-bye to parents/guardians).
8:45	Gathering time (discuss current project topic and activities of the day, read a book, sing songs).
9:00	Interest area/Project time (time to choose activities in interest areas and work on project-related activities individually and in small groups).
10:00	Outdoor play (time to choose outdoor activities, including trikes and playground equipment, if available. If weather does not permit going outside, children should have the opportunity to choose large motor activities indoors).
10:30	Snack (opportunity to enjoy time together with rich conversations).
10:45	Interest area/Project time.
11:15	Read a big book to the group, ask children to share what they did during the morning, and sing songs together.
11:30	Children go home or get ready for lunch.
11:45	Lunch.
12:15	Outdoor play.
12:45	Quiet time (looking at books, resting on mats).
1:15	Interest area/Project time as children are finished resting (others can remain asleep).
2:30	Read, sing songs, do movement activities.
2:45	Outdoor play.
3:30	Snack.
3:45	Interest areas, project-related activities, and small groups.
5:00	Closing (share and record together new discoveries of the day, plan for tomorrow, sing closing songs, choose from quiet activities until parents/guardians arrive).

Summary

It is important to create a welcoming environment where all children feel comfortable, safe, and excited to learn. Building warm, caring relationships with children will enhance their sense of self-worth and attitudes toward learning. Creating a community feeling built on mutual respect will add to the environment. Forming partnerships with parents increases benefits for children and their learning potential. The room can be arranged into interest areas where children can investigate and create with a variety of materials. Giving children the power to choose which interest areas to explore and how long to spend in each area increases children's motivation and independence. Interest areas provide children with the opportunity and time to learn and practice new skills. Plan large blocks of time in the day for children to become involved in interest areas and learn through their play. Include time in the schedule for reading, physical activity, music and movement, and time to explore projects and themes. Each moment of the day provides opportunities to share with children, talking, singing, playing, and learning together.

3

Developing Positive Approaches to Learning and Social-Emotional Development

hildren form attitudes toward learning very early in life. If they have positive experiences with learning and school, they are likely to view them as enjoyable and something they want to continue. However, if they have negative experiences and see learning as something unpleasant, they are more likely to try to avoid it.

Social-emotional development is an essential element of children's overall growth. The early years form the foundation that will be the basis of all future development. Relationships that children experience in the early years are crucial to their later social and emotional competence. Forming secure relationships with teachers and caregivers will support children's positive development and learning. To build these secure attachments, children need adults to respond to them and meet their needs. This attachment is like a dance between the child and the adult, with each one communicating and responding to the other. We need to spend quality time with children in our care, responding to their interests and needs, listening and talking with them. As we do this, children will see themselves as worthwhile and capable of learning.

Children need warm, responsive, inviting environments. It is our responsibility to provide an environment that is calm, predictable, positive, and stable, with appropriate expectations based on the children's ages and developmental levels. Enjoyable play experiences can help children develop pride, joy, and mastery of skills. As children play, they learn appropriate ways to express their emotions, self-regulation, turn taking, sharing, and negotiation. Play also helps children try on new roles and gain empathy for others' points of view.

Social-emotional development influences all areas of children's growth. Children who have a positive sense of self, good problem-solving skills, and positive approaches to learning are able to apply those competencies to their work with mathematics, science, and other academic areas. Helping children understand emotions is important for several other reasons:

- They are more likely to be sympathetic toward others and help others who are in distress.
- They are more likely to share what they have with others.
- They are generally more socially competent.
- Preschool children who understand others' feelings have better academic and social outcomes (Hyson, 2004).

Children who develop social and emotional competence in their early years are much more likely to demonstrate it in later years as well.

What Research and the Experts Tell Us
Approaches to Learning

Children's positive approaches to learning set the stage for later academic success and are a vital ingredient of school readiness. Children who enter kindergarten with enthusiasm, initiative, persistence, inventiveness, curiosity, problem-solving ability, and other learning behaviors are more able to take advantage of educational opportunities. These characteristics are not just inborn; children develop them over time in a supportive environment. (Hyson, in press)

Preschool standards in the areas of approaches to learning and social-emotional development describe skills that will lay the groundwork for children to be successful in all areas of development.

Sample Early Learning Guidelines for Approaches to Learning

STANDARD 1 ~ Curiosity and Eagerness

Children demonstrate curiosity and eagerness in play and everyday tasks.

STANDARD 2 ~ Initiative and Persistence

Children demonstrate initiative and persistence in play and everyday tasks.

STANDARD 3 ~ Problem Solving and Reflection

Children use problem solving and reflection in play and everyday tasks.

STANDARD 4 ~ Invention and Imagination

Children use invention and imagination in play and everyday tasks.

Sample Early Learning Guidelines for Social-Emotional Development

STANDARD 1 ~ Self-Concept and Self-Confidence

Children demonstrate a positive self-concept and self-confidence in play and everyday tasks.

STANDARD 2 ~ Regulating Emotions

Children demonstrate an ability to understand and regulate their emotions in play and everyday tasks.

STANDARD 3 ~ Respect and Appreciation of Similarities and Differences

Children respect others and recognize and appreciate their similarities and differences in play and everyday tasks.

STANDARD 4 ~ Pro-Social Behaviors and Cooperation

Children demonstrate pro-social behaviors and social competence and participate cooperatively as members of a group in play and everyday tasks.

Developing Positive Approaches to Learning and Social-Emotional Development Through Projects

The Project Approach is a wonderful way for children to develop a positive outlook on learning as they enjoy exploring new projects. Choosing a topic that appeals to both you and the children is a way to share common interests. Project topics that deal with learning about themselves, their families, and their communities are especially good at helping children learn about their emotions and developing their social skills.

As children investigate project topics, they can also be developing very positive approaches to learning. You may observe children noticing birds while outside at play:

"I love birds. Especially when they come, I love them."

"I like parrots. Parrots like to live by Animal Junction, and things about mourning doves I like is they have the same speed as other birds."

This may spark additional conversations and interest that lead to a project on birds. The project could focus on answering children's questions, such as how fast birds can fly. You could also pose a problem for the children to solve: "How could we help our bird friends we see flying by each day? What do you think they might need?" The group may decide to build a birdhouse from wood. They could work cooperatively on a creative design plan for the birdhouse and then work on the actual construction of the house. They could find ways to feed the birds and provide a water source for them. Working on a project gives children the opportunity to develop a sense of self-worth as they investigate, find answers, and share their new knowledge with others.

What Research and the Experts Tell Us
Social-Emotional Development

Research has shown that for children to be successful in school, they need skills in social and emotional areas as well as in academic areas. Children need to be able to communicate effectively, follow directions and cooperate, be attentive, enthusiastic, actively involved in classroom activities, and able to ask for and receive help (Pianta, 2002).

Marilou Hyson (2004) has outlined the basics of emotional understandings that are helpful for children to know:

Everyone has emotions....

Emotions arise because of different situations....

There are different ways of showing feelings....

Other people may not feel the same way I do about everything....

I can do things to change how I feel and how others feel.... (p. 53)

Designing the Environment

The design of our rooms can make a significant difference in children's approach to learning and their social-emotional development. Children need an atmosphere in which they feel comfortable, successful, and happy. An environment with interesting materials will inspire children's imaginations and encourage them to try new experiences and ask questions. Offer areas where children can be creative and learn to cooperate with others:

- *Art Area,* where children can explore a variety of art processes
- *Science Area,* where children can investigate and learn how things work
- *Block Area,* where children can build imaginative structures
- *Library Area,* where children can look at books that depict a variety of people and cultures

- *Dramatic Play Area,* where children can investigate a variety of roles, learn about the emotions of others, and develop social skills

Addressing Standards Through Engaging Experiences and Activities

The remainder of this chapter will present sample benchmarks for each of the approaches to learning and social-emotional standards, as well as activities to help children grow in these areas. These activities can be done in the context of a project or theme or used independently. Knowing children's individual levels of development will allow adults to intentionally plan appropriate, engaging experiences, such as those presented below, to help preschool children at all levels make progress.

Part I: Approaches to Learning

STANDARD 1 ~ Curiosity and Eagerness

Children demonstrate curiosity and eagerness in play and everyday tasks.

Benchmarks

By the end of their preschool years, most children will

1. Choose to participate in a wide variety of activities and demonstrate willingness to try new experiences

2. Ask questions to find answers and wonder why

3. Demonstrate eagerness to find out more about other people and to discover new things in their environment

Promoting Curiosity and Eagerness

Arrange the environment with interesting materials that will motivate children to try new experiences. Combine familiar activities and materials with new ones to help children ease into them. Give children time to observe new activities before joining in if they are hesitant. Set out materials in unusual ways that beckon children to play with them and lead them to explore new possibilities. Try putting blocks in the Housekeeping Area and dolls in the Block Area. Add soup ladles and large seashells to the sand and water tables. Hide small plastic insects, bears, or vehicles in the sand table and ask children to try finding them with plastic tongs. Add textures to paints at the easel with coffee grounds, glitter, or sand. Provide paper in interesting shapes, sizes, and colors in the Art and Writing Areas.

Engage in rich conversations with children throughout the day, discussing their ideas, interests, questions, and concerns. Encourage children to have conversations with each other in which they ask questions of one another, share, and compare ideas. Read stories about interesting people and places and encourage children to ask questions.

Set out dried corn and bean seeds for planting experiments. Provide a variety of materials for children to place them on, including sponges, paper towels, pie pans, construction paper, fabric, and other materials the children suggest.

Ask children to put the seeds on the different surfaces and then ask if they should add anything else if they want the seeds to grow. If children propose adding water, provide them with spray bottles they can use each day to water the seeds. Help children document the growth of the seeds on each different kind of material by measuring and drawing pictures weekly and adding these to a chart.

If you are able to get dried corn on the cob, try placing the whole ear of corn on a shallow pan of soil and invite children to water it when the soil feels dry. Ask children to draw pictures each week as the corn begins to sprout. Take photographs weekly as well and display them in the form of a time line, labeling each week.

STANDARD 2 ~ Initiative and Persistence

Children demonstrate initiative and persistence in play and everyday tasks.

Benchmarks

By the end of their preschool years, most children will

1. Demonstrate persistence by working toward completing tasks, and sustain attention and focus on activities

2. Select and engage in activities, moving independently from one activity to another, and demonstrate self-direction when making choices

3. Demonstrate self-help skills, including selecting toys and materials to use in activities and returning them when finished

Promoting Initiative

Arrange the room into interest areas where children can make choices about which materials to use and how long to spend using them. Keeping supplies on low shelves that are labeled makes it possible for children to find what they need and put things away on their own. Allow for plenty of time for children to explore materials and play, both inside

and outside. Encourage children to thoroughly explore activities and materials and complete tasks they have started. Plan the day to include a variety of learning experiences for both individuals and small groups. Make certain that there are activities appropriate for each child's interests and developmental level.

Plan engaging activities and experiences that will capture the children's attention and help them develop their ability to concentrate and persevere at a task. Visit interesting places in the neighborhood, including museums and parks, if available. Add intriguing objects to interest areas around the room. Provide a variety of materials to work with in each area that will encourage children to spend more time and become immersed in their efforts. Leave materials out for extended periods of time and encourage children to "keep trying just a little longer," when appropriate, to promote persistence.

STANDARD 3 ~ Problem Solving and Reflection

Children use problem solving and reflection in play and everyday tasks.

Benchmarks

By the end of their preschool years, most children will

1. Attempt several different strategies when encountering difficulty during daily routines or in the use of materials
2. Demonstrate satisfaction or delight when solving a problem or completing a task
3. Demonstrate thinking skills and verbal problem-solving skills (use self-talk and thinking aloud to solve problems)
4. Demonstrate resiliency and coping skills when faced with challenges
5. Seek help from adults and peers when needed

Promoting Problem Solving and Reflection

Teach children the steps involved in problem solving. Talk out loud while you solve problems or work through a task to model the problem-solving process. Encourage children to talk out loud as they work through an undertaking as well. Assist children in using conflict resolution skills as they are working through difficulties with other children. Encourage them to talk about the problem and negotiate solutions. Coach children through problem-solving steps as they face challenges, and then acknowledge and celebrate when children successfully solve a problem or complete a task.

Problem-Solving Steps

1. *Identify the problem:* What is the problem?
2. *Brainstorm possible solutions:* What can we do?
3. *Choose a solution:* What's the best choice to try?
4. *Try out the solution:* Let's try it.
5. *Evaluate how well the solution worked and choose another solution if needed:* Did it work? If not, what else shall we try?

Support children's efforts, providing just enough help for them to continue on their own. Have a range of materials with varying skill levels and challenges available. Let children know you are there to help with difficulties they may have and encourage them to ask friends for help as well. Promote reflection by asking children open-ended questions as they work. Build time in the day for reflection, such as during snack time, to talk about the day's events. Assist them in finding ways to overcome difficulties, which could include moving away from the situation, holding a favorite toy, or seeking comfort from an adult. Help children view mistakes as opportunities to learn, letting them know it is okay to make mistakes and giving them suggestions on how to remedy the situation.

STANDARD 4 ~ Invention and Imagination

Children use invention and imagination in play and everyday tasks.

Benchmarks

By the end of their preschool years, most children will

1. Explore and experiment with a wide variety of materials and activities

2. Make independent decisions about materials to use in order to express individuality

3. Develop creative solutions in play and daily situations

4. Engage in fantasy play, taking on pretend roles with real or imaginary objects

5. Use imagination to try new ways of doing things and work with materials in creative ways

Promoting Invention and Imagination

Expand broad, creative thinking by asking open-ended questions: "What would happen if . . . ?" "Why do you think . . . ?" "What could we do . . . ?" Accept children's responses and don't look for one "right" answer. Their divergent responses are the heart of creative thinking. Demonstrate your own creativity and willingness to try new ideas, activities, materials, and foods. Make certain that children have large blocks of time to play and independently select materials and activities.

Create an atmosphere that encourages children to use their imaginations while exploring fascinating materials. Add interest into the environment by introducing fish and other living things. Suspend prisms and items from the ceiling that twirl in the wind. Provide a variety of art materials that children can use creatively and encourage them to use materials in unique ways. Change materials and rotate toys and equipment periodically to give children new experiences and spark new ideas. Encourage divergent thinking by combining unusual items, such as adding fabrics to the Block Area. Introduce new items to the Housekeeping and Block Areas to expand play, including toys and objects that relate to the theme or project they are involved in.

Part II: Social-Emotional Development

STANDARD 1 ~ Self-Concept and Self-Confidence

Children demonstrate a positive self-concept and self-confidence in play and everyday tasks.

Benchmarks

By the end of their preschool years, most children will

1. Identify themselves by name

2. Describe themselves using several basic descriptors, such as gender and physical features

3. Take pride in accomplishments

4. Adjust to new situations

5. Separate easily from family members or familiar caregivers

6. Demonstrate self-efficacy by exerting independence in play situations and during regular routines

Promoting Self-Concept and Self-Confidence

Encourage independence by allowing children to choose activities and interest areas that are developmentally appropriate for them. Provide familiar, authentic materials for children's play, including real pots and pans, telephones, and safe woodworking tools and goggles. Make sure there are always activities available for children to do when they've finished something. To help children feel secure and know what to expect, establish a predictable daily routine. For children who have difficulty separating from parents, create an area near the entryway where children can play with familiar, engaging toys and materials until they feel comfortable moving on to other activities. Spend time with these children and help them join in play with others. Prepare children for new events or situations by explaining what will take place; show pictures or read books that might help children know what to expect. Create quiet, protected spaces where children can retreat, rest, and rejuvenate.

Recognize children's accomplishments by talking with individual children about what they have done and why they have reason to be proud. Display children's work at their eye level, along with their personal descriptions of the work.

Honor children and their names. Talk about what is special about each child in the group. During sharing time, encourage children to name positive characteristics of each other. Assist children in learning to print their names and identify them as their own. Encourage children to sign their names on art they have created. Label storage cubbies, lockers, or individual spaces with children's names. Invite families to bring in photographs of their families to display in the room. Ask children to identify themselves in the photographs and use words to describe themselves. When children arrive, greet each child and spend some individual time with each one during the day demonstrating your value and respect for them.

Share books about different kinds of families and encourage children to talk about their families. Read books illustrating positive role models for boys and girls.

STANDARD 2 ~ Regulating Emotions

Children demonstrate an ability to understand and regulate their emotions in play and everyday tasks.

Benchmarks

By the end of their preschool years, most children will

1. Use words to express their needs, wants, and feelings, as well as to identify the emotions of others

2. Demonstrate knowledge that there are different ways of showing feelings

3. Recognize they can do things to change the way they feel and how others feel

Promoting Regulating Emotions

Use puppets and dolls to help children talk about their emotions. Help children think about the causes of their emotions and appropriate ways to respond. Make use of puppets to explain different emotions and to teach children words to describe how they feel. Also, use everyday situations to discuss feelings and illustrate how their actions affect the feelings of others. Be aware of what children are feeling and provide guidance and support. Throughout the day, model how to express emotions in socially acceptable ways.

Coach children on how to use relaxation skills, including taking deep breaths. Teach children how to tighten and then relax muscles throughout their bodies, beginning with the face and progressing down to the feet. Demonstrate how to count slowly before reacting to challenges.

Give children words to use in a variety of situations. Role-play scenarios in small groups; ask children to use words to express their feelings as they encounter various circumstances. This could include someone taking toys they are playing with or wanting something that another child is using. Model words to use to help others feel better as well, such as offering to help when another child has fallen or been hurt.

STANDARD 3 ~ Respect and Appreciation of Similarities and Differences

Children respect others and recognize and appreciate their similarities and differences in play and everyday tasks.

Benchmarks

By the end of their preschool years, most children will

1. Express ways in which others are similar and different, such as eye color, gender, and favorite activities

2. Play with a variety of children, regardless of gender, race, or ability

3. Recognize that everyone has emotions and that other people may not feel the same way they do about everything

4. Demonstrate caring and concern for others

5. Respect the rights and property of others

Promoting Respect and Appreciation of Similarities and Differences

Create an environment that promotes respect, caring, and friendship. Plan periods of time during the day for children to play together in small groups, to encourage a variety of friendships. Take time in the day to talk individually with children, letting them know you are interested in them personally. Invite family members and individuals from the neighborhood to share their cultures and ways they contribute to the community. Involve children in activities that help the community, such as recycling, visiting the elderly, and collecting food or other items for those in need.

Make graphs with the children that include children's eye and hair color, gender, favorite foods, as well as other preferences and characteristics. Children can indicate the column they belong in with a picture of themselves, their names, or simply an X (see Table 3.1).

Add diversity to the graph by including favorite characters from storybooks. This is especially helpful to support children who might be the "only" child with certain characteristics, such as eyeglasses, a particular skin color, or one type of family configuration.

Use puppets or dolls to illustrate how to respect others, their personal space, and their property. As you play with the children, have the puppets demonstrate that other people have feelings and talk about how these feelings can be different from their own.

Table 3.1   Characteristics Graph

Brown Hair	Black Hair	Blond Hair
	Shawna	
	José	Patty
Jay	Catrina	Hugo
Carlos	Anthony	Andrew
Bridget	Pablo	Zuska

Books and music can help children learn about similarities and differences. Books such as *Two Eyes, a Nose, and a Mouth* and *All the Colors of the Earth* celebrate our similarities and differences. Stock the Library Area with books that depict a variety of cultures and traditions. Talk about the characters in favorite storybooks, discussing their feelings, similarities and differences in their appearances, and where they live. While children are playing, listen to music from a variety of cultures.

STANDARD 4 ~ Pro-Social Behaviors and Cooperation

Children demonstrate pro-social behaviors and social competence, and participate cooperatively as members of a group in play and everyday tasks.

Benchmarks

By the end of their preschool years, most children will

1. Develop positive relationships with peers and trusted adults

2. Participate in group routines and transition smoothly from one activity to the next

3. Use materials purposefully and respectfully and participate in cleaning up and putting away materials

4. Defend self while respecting the rights of others

5. Identify qualities that make a good friend

6. Play independently, in pairs, and cooperatively in small groups

7. Initiate play and know how to enter into a group of children who are already involved in play

8. Take turns, share, and be courteous to others, using words such as "thank-you," "please," and "excuse me"

Promoting Pro-Social Behaviors and Cooperation

Develop a sense of community among the children and adults in your setting by singing favorite songs, talking, and playing together. Work on establishing a personal relationship with every child in your care. Listen to them and let them know you care about them. Participate in activities with children, read to them, and have meaningful conversations. Join in their play, being respectful of cultural and individual preferences. Respond to children when they have needs and establish a sense of security and trust. Allow plenty of time during the day for children and adults to have enjoyable interactions, including routine times such as snack time, hand-washing, and cleanup. Avoid hurrying children.

Create transition routines that let everyone know they need to clean up or come to the circle. This could be designating a special song that you sing or play. Children then know they need to try to be finished by the time the song ends. Arrange the room so children can access materials easily. Use child-sized equipment and labeled shelves children can easily access to promote the ability to thoughtfully choose materials and return them when they are finished. Have enough supplies and toys available so children can play cooperatively.

Provide children with suggestions on how to be a good friend. Demonstrate how they can ask another child to play, or join play activities with another child or group of children, such as sharing toys and play ideas, offering to help, and giving compliments. Play games and do activities with the children that will help them learn turn taking and sharing in positive and fun ways. This might include cooking together, where everyone takes a turn adding ingredients and sharing. Plan plenty of time during the day for children to play together in groups of various sizes to help them develop friendships. Model good manners when interacting with the children and other adults. Acknowledge children when they use good manners, such as saying "please," "thank-you," and "excuse me" and holding the door for a friend. Become aware of cultural practices of the children in your care to ensure that you are being sensitive to their customs. Read books that demonstrate caring and being a good friend, such as *Friends* and *Making Friends*.

Supporting Children Who Are Bilingual Learners

Positive approaches to learning and a healthy self-concept can assist children as they try to learn a new language. It is important that children feel comfortable and accepted and know that it is all right to take chances and make mistakes. Correcting their speaking errors may cause them to lose interest in trying. Instead, we can provide good models for them and encourage and support their efforts through a variety of activities:

- Learn key words and phrases in the children's languages so you can communicate basic messages with them, including words of affection and approval. Encourage them to use their home languages as well as the new words they are learning in English.
- Get to know children as individuals, understanding their needs and interests.
- Engage in genuine conversations with the children throughout the day, including snack time and mealtime.
- Provide many opportunities for children to talk with other children and adults as they play.
- Help children learn words they need for basic communication and self-help.
- Encourage children to feel comfortable asking others to repeat words or directions they do not understand or to ask about the meaning of words they don't know.
- Encourage children to dictate stories about themselves, their families, and their friends.

- Decorate with fabrics and other artifacts that reflect the cultures of the families and community.
- Invite family members to join in activities, such as making a personal book for each child. This book could be made from construction paper, paper plates, or ziplock bags. Each page or bag can contain something meaningful about the child. The first page might contain a picture of the child and a card with his or her name. Subsequent pages could have words and pictures or objects to describe favorite colors, games, books, toys, songs, or seasons. Families could help children make similar books about their families at another time.

Working With Children's Individual Needs

It is important that all children in our programs feel successful and capable. For this to occur, we may need to make adaptations to our environment and activities so that each child can participate fully. If a child is having any kind of difficulty, the first question to ask is what is causing the problem? Are there physical, emotional, social, cognitive, or communication delays or some other contributing factors? Finding the cause will often lead to possible solutions. Many of the following suggestions will be helpful for all children in our programs:

- Establish an environment that makes it possible for all children to actively participate and be successful, including interest areas where all children can easily access materials and activities. Allowing children to move freely, choose activities, and talk with one another may decrease challenging behaviors caused by children needing to sit still and wait quietly. This active engagement will also promote motivation, attention, and learning.
- Acknowledge children's attempts and positive behaviors.
- Use carpet squares, rugs, or fabric to designate workspaces for the materials children use for various activities.
- Prepare the environment so children feel calm, happy, and safe. For children who are easily overstimulated, eliminate excessive clutter or room displays.
- Make transitions easier for children by alerting them as to how much time is left before a transition will occur: "There are 5 minutes left before we need to clean up . . . 3 minutes . . . 1 more minute." Designate special songs for transitions that help children know what is expected, such as a song to sing when it is time to come inside.
- To help children anticipate the activities of the day, use pictures or photographs to display a daily schedule. Provide pictures or photos of activities and materials for children who have difficulty communicating with words.
- Write social stories with individuals or small groups that portray children facing challenges similar to their own and dealing with them in positive ways.
- Create partnerships with families to work together to meet children's individual needs.
- Access community resource people to provide additional support for children and families.

The Resources section at the back of this book includes Web sites and other materials that provide more information and additional support.

Summary

When children have positive approaches toward learning, they are able to get more out of experiences, enjoy time spent in these activities, have better attitudes, and learn more. These approaches to learning encompass the areas of curiosity, eagerness, initiative, problem solving, reflection, invention, and imagination. Children's social-emotional development is also critical to learning, social interactions, and quality of life. Early learning guidelines for the social-emotional area include self-concept, self-confidence, and regulation of emotions; respect and appreciation of similarities and differences; and pro-social behaviors and cooperation. Exploring project topics can help children develop problem solving, good approaches to learning, and sound social-emotional growth. The environment should invite children to try new experiences, seek answers to their questions, and be actively involved in play and learning.

Exploring the World Through Science

Through science, children begin to understand their world and can develop genuine curiosity and positive approaches to learning. One of our primary goals for our children's learning and development is to help them establish a sense of wonder about the world around them. Rachel Carson expressed it beautifully in her book *The Sense of Wonder* (1965), when she wrote,

> If I had influence with the good fairy, who is supposed to preside over the christening of all children, I should ask that her gift to each child in the world be a sense of wonder so indestructible that it would last throughout life. (p. 43)

We can promote this wonder by setting up opportunities for children to explore, ask questions, and learn. Science experiences are a wonderful way to help children to begin to understand their environment. Through science, children can learn to appreciate and take care of their surroundings and develop respect for all living things.

What Research and the Experts Tell Us
Young Children and Science

Young children are natural scientists. They have great enthusiasm for investigating the world around them and a need to make sense of their world (Chalufour & Worth, 2003; Chrisman, 2005). Science can be integrated throughout the curriculum in the early years and can form a backdrop for children's learning in language, mathematics, and social skills (Worth & Grollman, 2003). The National Research Council report *Eager to Learn: Educating Our Preschoolers* (Bowman, Donovan, & Burns, 2000) states that observations and predictions are the foundations of scientific inquiry. Curriculum for young children should include opportunities to observe and predict through hands-on, meaningful activities and discovery centers where children explore and investigate (Chrisman, 2005; Colker, 2002).

Preschool science standards outline knowledge and skills that young children can develop through hands-on activities and exploration. Below are sample preschool science standards, based on the categories designated by the National Science Education Standards. It is important for adults to support children as they develop their understanding of science concepts over time and celebrate beginning steps. If a child describes melting ice as "It magic'd," we can acknowledge that the child has seen the transformation: "It did change didn't it! It melted. What is it like now?"

Sample Early Learning Guidelines for Science

Standard 1 ~ Science as Inquiry

As a result of their explorations and participation in simple investigations through play, children demonstrate their understanding of and ability to use scientific inquiry.

Standard 2 ~ Physical Science

As a result of their explorations and participation in simple investigations through play, children develop an understanding of properties, position, and motion of objects in the environment.

Standard 3 ~ Life Science

As a result of their explorations and participation in simple investigations through play, children develop an understanding of characteristics, life cycles, and environments of living things.

Standard 4 ~ Earth and Space Science

As a result of their explorations and participation in simple investigations through play, children develop an understanding of properties of earth materials, objects in the sky, and changes in the earth and sky.

Standard 5 ~ Science and Technology

As a result of their explorations and participation in simple investigations through play, children develop an understanding about science and technology and the ability to distinguish between natural objects and objects made by humans.

Standard 6 ~ Science, Environment, and Society

As a result of their explorations and participation in simple investigations through play, children demonstrate an awareness of and respect for the environment and how it can be changed. Children demonstrate an understanding that people use science to explore the world and answer questions.

SOURCE: Reprinted with permission from *National Science Education Standards*, © 1996, by the National Academy of Sciences, courtesy of the National Academies Press, Washington, DC.

Exploring the World and Science Through Projects

Long-term projects, or focused studies, with science themes can help children learn not only about their world and concepts of science; they can also learn literacy, mathematics, and other content areas in a meaningful context. Observe children at play. What fascinates them? Do they enjoy exploring water and sand? Are they interested in rocks, dirt, plants, bugs, or other animals? What experiences intrigue them during the different times of the year in your area? Listen to their conversations:

"We saw baby chicks at the farm."

"Yeah, and they were yellow—and they had feathers!"

"They had three claws, and they were sharp!"

"They were soft."

"They said 'peep, peep.'"

"They were saying 'hello.'"

Children's interests can become good starting points for projects or focused studies and can provide multiple opportunities for children to learn.

In a project on baby chicks, trees, or other nature-related topics, children will be meeting many of the science standards, as well as standards in many other curriculum areas, in an authentic, meaningful way. Through field trips, observations, and seeing pictures in captivating books, they will be able to begin to classify living things as animals or plants and use words to describe them, as these words are used throughout the project. They will experience firsthand that living things have basic needs, such as food, water, and air, by caring for baby chicks or planting small trees or seeds. They will recognize that living things change and grow throughout their life cycles because they will be seeing it themselves.

Through projects, children can learn ways to represent what they are observing and learning. They could participate in making a mural depicting what they saw or discovered through their investigations. In a project on trees, the mural might include paintings of trees they learned about, along with the rain and sun the trees need to survive. Children could also paint individual pictures, draw, make representations out of play dough or clay, make a collage, or dramatize their learning through movement, dance, and song.

Designing the Environment

Setting up a Science/Discovery Area in the room is an excellent way to provide opportunities for children to explore. The area would ideally be located near a window, allowing children to observe both outdoors and indoors. The window would also provide natural light for growing plants. The Discovery/Science Area could include low tables or

shelves that the children can easily access. This area can encompass all areas of science and could include materials such as the following:

Balance scale

Magnifying glasses

Magnets

Objects from nature, such as leaves, pinecones, rocks, and shells

Classroom pets

Aquarium

Growing plants

Prisms and kaleidoscopes

Child-safe thermometer

Pulleys, gears, wheels, and inclined planes

Books on science-related topics

Addressing Standards Through Engaging Experiences and Activities

While enhancing our curriculum to help children meet standards and benchmarks, we need to make sure that children are given opportunities to learn science concepts through play and exploration, using hands-on materials. The following section presents sample benchmarks for each preschool science standard, along with suggestions to help children learn them through developmentally appropriate, engaging activities. The activities can be used in the context of a long-term project or theme or used individually.

STANDARD 1 ~ Science as Inquiry

As a result of their explorations and participation in simple investigations through play, children demonstrate their understanding of and ability to use scientific inquiry.

Benchmarks

By the end of their preschool years, most children will

1. Express wonder, ask questions, and make simple predictions, such as whether an object will sink or float.

2. Observe and use senses to explore materials and their environment both indoors and outdoors.

3. Use simple tools and measuring devices, such as balance scales, thermometers, and rulers to explore the environment.

Promoting Science as Inquiry

Provide opportunities for children to experience concepts firsthand by walking outside and observing the world around them. Encourage children to use their senses:

- *Feel* the wind in their hair and the warmth of the sun on their skin
- *Listen* for birds and other nature sounds
- *Look* for nests, butterflies, birds, and spiderwebs
- *Touch* sand, rocks, and soil
- *Smell* flowers and scents in the air and try to identify where the smells might be coming from

Consider asking children to notice details, such as new buds on trees and the petals on a flower. Bring objects from nature inside for further exploration and encourage children to use magnifying glasses to take a closer look at leaves, small twigs, pinecones, and blades of grass. When walking outside isn't possible, bring the outdoors in through vivid pictures, photographs, books, and posters.

Provide a water table or container of water and have children predict whether objects will sink or float, and then try out their predictions. At other times, provide funnels, measuring cups, and spoons that children can use to explore and play with the water.

Offer opportunities for exploration and wonder. Set up simple experiments and experiences for children throughout the day. For example, fill water bottles with a variety of liquids. One bottle could have water, another vegetable oil, and another corn syrup. Invite children to drop a marble in each bottle and securely close the cap. Children can then observe how long it takes the marble to fall through each type of liquid. Encourage children to ask questions, make predictions, and suggest other liquids to explore, such as shampoo, milk, or liquid soap. Help children test their predictions with these liquids as well.

Because children enjoy using measuring tools in their play, balance scales should have a permanent home in the Science Area, where children can pursue their own investigations through play on a daily basis. As children compare the weight of objects, occasionally ask them to predict which will be heavier before they try it out. Then, help the children record their predictions and findings. This can be done on a large sheet of paper, divided into two columns: *Heavier* and *Lighter.* Have children tell you which object they think will be heavier, and then you write the predictions in the appropriate columns or have them draw pictures of the objects. After children use the balance scale to find out which object is indeed heavier, they can compare their results with their predictions.

Children also enjoy measuring objects with rulers and measuring tapes, which they can do both indoors and outside. With assistance, they can chart the growth of classroom plants over time on a large sheet of paper that is displayed for all to see. They can also measure with nonstandard objects, such as paper clips, blocks, string, or toy cars. Help children use safe thermometers to measure air temperature as well as the temperature of other materials, such as containers of water. Encourage the children to observe whether the red line of the thermometer is going up or down and describe the temperature as "warm" or "cold."

STANDARD 2 ~ Physical Science

As a result of their explorations and participation in simple investigations through play, children develop an understanding of properties and motion of objects in the environment.

Benchmarks

By the end of their preschool years, most children will

1. Observe and use words to describe physical changes, such as a solid turning to liquid

2. Identify similarities and differences of objects

3. Compare and sort materials according to one or more properties

4. Explore ways to move objects, such as pushing or pulling, and describe these motions

Promoting Physical Science

Observe the physical changes that take place when you make gelatin with the children. Watch as it changes from powder, to a liquid mixture, and then to a solid. Children can also observe these changes as they participate in cooking and baking activities or making play dough.

Children can explore physical science at the water table, or with a large plastic container of water. Put ice and/or snow in the water table occasionally for children to observe. You could also ask children to place individual portions of ice or snow in various parts of the room, including the water table, and notice differences in the amount of time it takes them to melt.

Make bubbles with the children and watch them pop.

Recipe for Bubbles

1 part liquid dish soap

10 parts water

Small amount of glycerin, if desired

Add 1 cup of liquid dish soap to 10 cups of water (any size cup or container could be used to measure, depending on the amount needed, as long as you maintain a 1:10 ratio). Add a small amount of glycerin, to add elasticity to the bubbles, if desired. Glycerin is available at many drugstores but is not a necessary ingredient. Allow mixture to age overnight or even a week or two for longer-lasting bubbles.

Items That Can Be Used as Bubble Wands

Pipe cleaners formed in various shapes

Plastic strawberry baskets

Thread spools

Plastic from six-pack beverage containers

New fly swatters

Plastic cottage cheese cartons with a small hole made in the bottom

Invite children to think of other items that could be used to make bubbles.

TRY THIS!

Create a picture graph with the children by taking photographs or helping them to take photos or draw objects they see outside. Then, use these photos or drawings to create a picture graph by putting them under appropriate headings, such as "Made of Wood," "Made of Metal," or "Made of Glass."

Provide a variety of toys children can use to investigate motion, including balls and toy vehicles. Encourage children to think of things they could use as ramps (inclined planes). Provide soup cans and other materials for children to use on the ramps. Encourage children to think of other objects they could attempt to roll down the ramp, as well as objects that do not roll. Take your investigations outdoors and use a slide or teeter-totter as the inclined plane.

Supply the Block Area with a variety of blocks, toy vehicles, and other materials children can use to build structures and explore motion. As children are playing, talk with them about their constructions, the position of the blocks, and similarities and differences in the items they are using. Encourage both boys and girls to spend time in the Block Area; making sure the area is appealing to all children. Give children the opportunity to sort blocks and other toys according to shape, size, or color. Furnish objects made of different types of materials, such as wood, metal, and paper, for children to sort.

STANDARD 3 ~ Life Science

As a result of their explorations and participation in simple investigations through play, children develop an understanding of characteristics, life cycles, and environments of living things.

Benchmarks

By the end of their preschool years, most children will

1. Observe and classify living things as animals or plants and use words to describe them

2. Demonstrate knowledge that living things have basic needs, such as food, water, and air

3. Demonstrate knowledge that plants, animals, and humans live in environments that support their needs, such as fish living in water

4. Recognize that living things, including themselves, change and grow throughout their life cycles

Promoting Life Science

Planting gardens with the children either inside or outside gives children opportunities to learn firsthand about the needs of plants and how they change and grow. Before planting a garden outside, research what grows well in your area and

Place plant cuttings in clear gel, available in home and garden stores, to allow children to see the roots as they develop. Children can also start seeds in clear plastic bags on wet paper towels and then transfer them to the gel once the seeds have sprouted.

Plant potatoes, radishes, beans, and lettuce in clear, 2-liter bottles. Place a removable piece of black construction paper around the outside of the bottle, surrounding the soil to shield the roots from sunlight when the children aren't viewing it. Adding a grow light will promote plant growth in rooms with little natural light.

When out on a walk, take a picture of a neighborhood tree. Use this photograph to make books by making a photocopy of the picture and duplicating it, so that each child can have a book with five pages, each including a photograph of the tree. (This could be the same picture of one tree or multiple trees. It could also be a picture from a magazine or hand drawn.) At the Science or Writing Area, ask each child to dictate a sentence for each page about what a tree needs to live and grow and then draw this idea on that page. For example, one page might read, "The tree needs water," and the next, "The tree needs sunshine," and so forth. Ask children to create titles for the cover pages of their books and write their names as the authors.

involve children in deciding what to plant. Gardens can be any shape or size and grown in a variety of containers, including plastic tubs, large flower pots, pails, plastic milk jugs, little red wagons, or almost any container. It is helpful to provide drainage by drilling holes in the bottom of the container and lining it with rocks or pebbles to keep the roots alive and healthy.

A classroom pet can teach children about animals, how they grow, and how to care for them. Guinea pigs and fish are good choices, although you must be sensitive to children's allergies, health regulations, and the well-being of the animals. Involve children in setting up a quality environment for the pet and talk about what it needs to survive and be comfortable in its new home. Invite parents or people in the community to bring in family pets, baby animals, or other animals that will provide children with additional experiences.

Taking walks outside gives children the opportunity to observe plants and animals and discuss their needs. Give children opportunities to play and enjoy being outside or set up an area inside where children can play with and explore natural objects. Talk informally with children, as they play, about the plants and animals living in their surroundings. Children enjoy looking for and finding insects. If children want to observe an insect more closely, talk with them about how to set up a good environment for the insect. Help children construct this environment, observe, and then release the insect at the end of the day or within a short period of time.

Have a scavenger hunt and ask children to look for plants and animals. On a piece of large chart paper, make two columns, one for *Plants* and one for *Animals*. Ask children to report their findings and decide which columns the items belong in. This could be done outside or inside, using books, posters and other items around the room. On another day, have a hunt for things that are "living" or "nonliving." Although this distinction is difficult for preschool-aged children, hands-on experiences will help them begin to understand the differences over time. Encourage children to discuss their thinking about this and support their attempts.

Make books with the children, showing them as babies and as they look today. Ask families to send in photographs of the children as infants or toddlers.

Trees need rain.

Trees need soil.

Take current photos of the children involved in activities. Make a book with two pages facing each other for each child. Attach the child's baby picture to one side of the book and the current picture on the other side. Include children's names and possibly a few easy-to-read lines, such as, "Miguel was a baby" and "Look at Miguel today!" Put a copy of the book in the Library Area, where children can enjoy it. With families' permission, make a copy of the book for each child to take home and share. You could also make similar books by using pictures of animals and their babies.

STANDARD 4 ~ Earth and Space Science

As a result of their explorations and participation in simple investigations through play, children develop an understanding of properties of earth materials, objects in the sky, and changes in the earth and sky.

Benchmarks

By the end of their preschool years, most children will

1. Explore the properties of earth materials, such as sand and water, through play
2. Name objects in the sky, including sun, moon, clouds, and stars
3. Describe differences between night and day
4. Recognize and describe current conditions and changes in the weather
5. Observe and describe basic changes in the seasons

Promoting Earth and Space Science

Provide opportunities for children to explore sand, soil, and water with a magnifying glass or child's microscope. Children could explore sand in a sand table or large container of sand, indoors or outside. They could add water to sand and soil, watch the changes that occur, and then mold the sand and water into various shapes.

Children can explore a variety of science concepts through art. Ask children to discover what happens when they dip their fingers in a bowl of water and allow water to drip onto a piece of colored tagboard or tissue paper. With large brushes and a bucket of water, children could paint a variety of surfaces outside, including walls and sidewalks, and watch as the water evaporates.

Take the art easel outside. Encourage children to observe the sky and their surroundings and then paint their observations.

Have fun cloud watching with the children and discussing what they are able to see in the day and night skies. Read *It Looked Like Spilt Milk*, a simple, predictable book about finding shapes in clouds. Encourage children to paint pictures similar to those found in the book, using white paint on blue construction paper. Children could also try putting a spoonful of white paint on the paper, folding the paper in half, and pressing to spread the paint. Have them dictate a sentence describing what the picture looks like. Read other books and sing songs about day and night, including "Day-O" and other favorite "good-morning" songs.

Play outside during different seasons, if possible, and discuss changes children observe. Talk about weather conditions as they occur, such as rain, thunder, and lightening. Read weather-related books, such as *Amy Loves the Wind*, and talk about what causes wind, thunder, and lightening to help alleviate any fears children may have.

STANDARD 5 ~ Science and Technology

As a result of their explorations and participation in simple investigations through play, children develop an understanding about science and technology and the ability to distinguish between natural objects and objects made by humans.

Benchmarks

By the end of their preschool years, most children will

1. Use tools or objects in the environment to solve problems or complete tasks

2. Use the computer and other technology, if available, to explore how their actions can cause an effect

3. Identify some objects as being found in nature and others as being made by people

Promoting Science and Technology

Ask children to find natural objects outdoors, such as pinecones, small twigs, rocks, or shells, or bring in items children can use. Invite them to make an imprint of the object in play dough that is flattened onto a plastic plate or margarine tub lid. Involve children in conversations about why some materials are natural and others are not. Bring in both real and artificial flowers for children to explore and discuss their differences.

Take photographs of natural objects outside to extend potential learning opportunities. These pictures can be displayed on posters, bulletin boards, or panels documenting children's work throughout the project. The photos can also be made into a book, with one photograph on each page, accompanied by words children dictate. Children could give the book a title such as *Look What We Found in Nature!*

Use good-quality, developmentally appropriate software if you have a computer available. There are Web sites that rate both children's software and Web sites, such as Children's Technology Review (http://www.childrenssoftware.com). Software is available that gives children access only to those programs you want them to use. Talk about the different ways the computer helps people and model ways to look up topics children are interested in. Give children the opportunity to type on the computer. This can be done using your regular word-processing program, with a large font, or a children's writing program. Occasionally record data from the children's experiments and other science experiences in a chart on the computer.

What Research and the Experts Tell Us
Young Children and Technology

Studies have shown that working on computers can have a positive impact on children's cognitive development and higher-order thinking skills. Playing together on computers can also promote cooperative learning and social skills. The key to these positive effects is the use of high-quality, developmentally appropriate software and Web sites (Clements, 1999; Haugland & Wright, 1997; Saracho & Spodek, 2003). Software should be developmentally appropriate for children and offer opportunities for creative play and problem solving. Software should promote positive social values and tolerance and portray positive representations of culture, linguistic diversity, physical abilities, and gender. Computers cannot, however, replace quality hands-on experiences and interactions with adults and other children (National Association for the Education of Young Children, 1996). More information on technology and young children can be found at http://www.techandyoungchildren.org.

Use a variety of tools with the children, such as a vegetable peeler, an apple-peeling machine, a flour sifter, an eggbeater, or even an ice cream maker. In the Woodworking Area, give children the opportunity to create structures with screwdrivers, hammers, and hand drills. Using these tools helps children learn about cause and effect and experience how their actions can cause something to happen. Always provide adult supervision and child safety glasses when offering woodworking experiences.

STANDARD 6 ~ Science, Environment, and Society

As a result of their explorations and participation in simple investigations through play, children demonstrate an awareness of and respect for the environment and how it can be changed. Children demonstrate an understanding that people use science to explore the world and answer questions.

Benchmarks

By the end of their preschool years, most children will

1. Demonstrate care and respect for the environment

2. Demonstrate knowledge that their actions and actions of others can change the environment

3. Recognize ways to recycle and reuse materials

4. Demonstrate understanding that everyone can use science to explore and solve problems

Promoting Science, Environment, and Society

Set up a recycling center in the room where children can put paper scraps and sort other recyclables. Children can then use some of this recycled paper in the Art Area, as well as paper towel rolls, plastic bottle caps, empty spools, and scraps of ribbon, yarn, and fabric to design new creations. Encourage children to use both sides of a sheet of paper and clean up their environment by clearing the table and picking up toys and litter. Opportunities to learn about recycling help children begin to understand that their actions, such as conserving resources, can make a difference.

Give children opportunities to demonstrate their respect for living things and the environment by caring for pets, respecting each other, and keeping their environment clean. Encourage both girls and boys to take part in science experiences. Emphasize that both boys and girls are good at science and that science is the way we find out about the world.

TRY THIS!

Make recycled paper with the children by providing newspaper in the Science Area that they can tear into small pieces. Help them pour water over the paper to soak overnight. The following day, pour the paper mixture into a blender and grind into pulp. Place an old window screen or other wire screen over a plastic container large enough to catch the water that will drip from the pulp. Pour the pulp into a thin layer on the screen, and use a sponge to smooth out the pulp and remove excess water. Allow the pulp to dry for several days. When it is dry, remove the recycled paper from the screen. Invite children to examine the recycled paper with a magnifying glass and draw on it with crayons. Children can also make recycled paper with scraps of used construction paper or other types of paper.

Supporting Children Who Are Bilingual Learners

Provide support for children who are learning English as a new language. Encourage them to use their home languages while learning new words in English. Science provides many interesting experiences that may provide motivation and opportunities to learn new words. These experiences will also give children background knowledge that they will be able to build on later to expand their vocabularies:

- Take walks outside with children and point out interesting objects in the environment. Emphasize the names of the objects and encourage children to find other examples, repeating the names of the objects if they are comfortable doing so. Focus on words that are useful and simple for the child.
- Take photographs with the children of flowers, trees, wheels, magnets, machines, places you've visited, or other things they find fascinating. Add words to label the photographs and hang them where children can enjoy and talk about them. Make science-related books with the children using these photographs or simple pictures

and words. Read the books frequently with the children and share them with their families.

- Ask children to work in pairs, allowing a child who speaks English well to help another who is learning to speak it. Encourage the partner to play, talk, and support the child who is learning English.
- Learn key words and phrases in the children's languages so that you can communicate basic messages with them. Encourage them to use their home languages as well as the new science words they are learning in English.
- Invite families to participate in science activities and fieldwork.
- Provide science activities that can easily be done without requiring children to speak until they are comfortable doing so.

Working With Children's Individual Needs

It is important in our work with children to make sure that we are addressing the needs of all children. Each child has unique characteristics, rates of development, and prior experiences that influence them. We need to adapt the curriculum to ensure that each child benefits as much as possible from learning experiences. There are several things we can consider that will allow all children to be successful:

- Design the environment so that every child can access materials in the Science Area. Some materials and activities can be moved to the floor or other areas that allow greater access for those who need it.
- Provide science experiences in a variety of settings, including different areas of the room and building, as well as outdoors.
- Place materials in plastic jars or bags to allow children who prefer not touching items to explore them.
- Add handles to measuring tools and science materials to make them easier for children to use independently.
- Use a modified keyboard or mouse, if needed, to make the computer accessible to all children.

Summary

The National Science Education Standards include the following areas: Science as Inquiry, Physical Science, Life Science, Earth and Space Science, Science and Technology, and Science, Environment, and Society. Preschool children can begin to develop an understanding of concepts involved in these areas through engaging projects and activities. Projects with science-related themes, such as trees, gardens, water, rocks, animals, and insects, allow children to learn science concepts as well as develop curiosity and wonder about the world. Science-related topics also provide a meaningful context for children to develop knowledge and skills in all other areas of the curriculum. Designing the environment with engaging materials and interest areas where children can explore science concepts both indoors and outdoors will also contribute to children's understanding of science standards.

5

Learning About Our Community Through Social Studies

Through social studies, children learn about families, neighborhoods, communities, and cultures. They learn about being good members of their families, groups, neighborhoods, and communities, which is the beginning of civics education. They develop a sense of history and time as they learn to identify yesterday, today, and tomorrow and recall things they have done in the past. Children learn skills they will need to understand geography as they have experiences that help them understand and use terms such as *near, far, over, under, here,* and *there.* They learn the beginnings of economics in the Dramatic Play Area when they set up a pretend store and make believe they are buying and selling goods.

What Research and the Experts Tell Us
Young Children and Social Studies

According to the National Council for the Social Studies (1993), "The primary purpose of social studies is to help young people develop the ability to make informed and reasoned decisions for the public good as citizens of a culturally diverse, democratic society in an interdependent world" (p. 3). Taking part in studies on topics such as food, clothing, families, or transportation can help children develop a sense of civic responsibility. The environment can support children's learning of social studies through learning centers, posters with children's questions and answers they have discovered, comfortable places to work as individuals and small groups, and hands-on activities (Mindes, 2005). To be effective, social studies needs to be meaningful, integrated with other subject areas, and based on topics of interest to the children (Seefeldt, 2001).

Preschool social studies standards outline knowledge and skills that young children can develop through exploration and meaningful experiences. Below are sample preschool standards for social studies.

Sample Early Learning Guidelines for Social Studies

STANDARD 1 ~ Families/Cultures

Through their explorations, play, and social interactions, children demonstrate an understanding of self, families, and cultures.

STANDARD 2 ~ Community/Civics

Through their explorations, play, and social interactions, children demonstrate an understanding of what it means to be a participating member of groups and communities.

STANDARD 3 ~ History/Time

Through their explorations, play, and social interactions, children demonstrate an understanding of the passage of time and how the past influences their future.

STANDARD 4 ~ Geography/Places, People, and Environments

Through their explorations, play, and social interactions, children demonstrate an awareness of their physical environment and its impact on daily living.

STANDARD 5 ~ Economics

Through their explorations, play, and social interactions, children demonstrate an understanding of how people work together to grow, produce, distribute, and consume goods and services that meet their wants and needs.

SOURCE: These standards have been adapted based on the following thematic strands of curriculum standards for social studies developed by the National Council for the Social Studies (NCSS): Culture; Civic Ideals and Practices; Individuals, Groups, and Institutions; Time, Continuity, and Change; People, Places, and Environment; and Production, Distribution, and Consumption. Complete information on all ten NCSS thematic strands is available in the publication *Expectations of Excellence: Curriculum Standards for Social Studies* (Washington, DC: National Council for the Social Studies, 1994). See also www .socialstudies.org.

Learning About Our Community and Social Studies Through Projects

Social studies, like science, offers rich possibilities for topics of study. A study of families, the neighborhood, clothes, transportation, or people and places in the community are worthy topics for projects. The Bank Street College of Education recommends using social studies themes as topics for focused studies throughout the year (D'Addesio, Grob, Furman, Hayes, & David, 2005; Mitchell & David, 1992).

In choosing a topic of study, observe children's interests. Children may talk about new construction in the neighborhood or their own apartments or homes:

Pedro: Look at that big machine digging in the dirt.

Kim: Yeah, that building there is getting really big.

Juan: My home has lots of rooms. Some of them I know, some I don't know. Mom's room, my sister's room, my room, the living room, and the kitchen. I guess I know all the rooms.

Kim: My room is my home. It has toys. My blanket, my kitty cat, and my bed. And my window too. I can see the rain.

The topic of homes would lend itself to interesting investigations if children have expressed curiosity about them. Build on this interest by providing a variety of blocks children could use for construction in the Block Area, as well as a variety of materials to use for designing homes in the Art Area. Stock the Library Area with books about homes similar to those in their neighborhoods and homes found around the world. Talk about the fact that some families do not live in a traditional "house," making sure that any children who may be homeless feel valued and accepted. Discuss the various types of homes in which children can live, including shelters, so that all children are involved.

Parents or community members could be invited to help design and construct a dollhouse for use in the program. Children could be involved in the design, construction, and interior decorating of the house. They could take part in discussions about rooms and furniture needed, how these could be constructed, and what materials could be used. This could continue throughout the year, as children make simple rugs, curtains, pillows, and other items for the house out of paper or cloth.

As part of the project, parents and community members could help design and build a playhouse for the children themselves. The playhouse could be either inside or outside, depending on your needs and the materials available. Children can be involved in the design and construction as well, under close supervision with adequate safety measures. The playhouse could be extremely simple and open or more elaborate depending on funds, materials, and help available. Parents and community members could also be asked to help build a piece of playground equipment. Children could be part of this construction process as well. Through this type of project, you will be addressing standards in all areas of the curriculum.

A sunflower house could be planted in spring or early summer. To do this, children could plant sunflower seeds around the perimeter of a small section of ground, about 4 to 8 feet square. Giant varieties of sunflowers provide a good height for the house. Other seeds, planted in between the giant sunflowers, add color and interest at the children's eye level. Children could take part in the decision of what other plants to add. Morning glory, cosmos, marigolds, beans, corn, peppermint, and chamomile all work well for this purpose.

Designing the Environment

The environment can convey powerful messages about what we value and what is important. Providing pictures, posters, and books that show diverse families, customs,

homes, and terrains can help children learn about a variety of cultures and environments. Send home disposable cameras families can use to take family photos that can be placed in frames around the room or hung at the children's eye level. These pictures can be scanned or photocopied and made into a book that can be stored in the classroom library. Tell parents and guardians how you would like to use the photographs and request their permission before using them.

Set up the environment with interest areas where children can play, giving them the opportunity to make choices and learn how to interact with each other. Include a Dramatic Play Area where children can try out a variety of roles, including family members and community helpers. Play music from many cultures that children can listen and move to as they play. Bring in instruments from a variety of cultures, such as rain-sticks, drums, and maracas for children to play.

Addressing Standards Through Engaging Experiences and Activities

We can plan opportunities throughout the day to help children learn social studies concepts through play and everyday experiences. The following section presents sample benchmarks for each social studies standard, along with suggestions to help preschool children of all ages learn them through developmentally appropriate, engaging activities. The activities can be used in the context of a long-term project or theme or used individually.

STANDARD 1 ~ Families/Cultures

Through their explorations, play, and social interactions, children demonstrate an understanding of self, families, and cultures.

Benchmarks

By the end of their preschool years, most children will

1. Identify themselves as individuals and as belonging to a family
2. Describe what a family is and roles that family members can play
3. Share family traditions and daily routines and demonstrate interest in learning about the traditions of others
4. Demonstrate understanding that there are diverse families and cultures and all have value

Promoting Understanding of Families/Cultures

Read books about many different types of families and cultures. Ask children to discuss what makes a family and what it means to be a good family member. Encourage children to discuss the makeup of their own families. Emphasize the importance of respecting and valuing all types of families and cultures. Read books and show pictures of different types of family structures, homes, and transportation. Talk with children about similarities and differences between their own communities and those around the world.

Invite family members, including parents, grandparents, aunts, and uncles, to share family customs, stories, music, dance, traditions, dress, and other items from their cultures. Ask families to help plan cultural celebrations throughout the year. Families can also bring in family recipes to share and help prepare with the children. These can be collected into a family recipe book to share with all the families in the program. Prepare foods from a variety of cultures for snacks and meals, such as tacos and latkes (potato pancakes).

Decorate the room with multicultural materials, such as fabrics from various cultures. Hang posters with pictures of children from around the world. Put clothes and dolls from various cultures in the Dramatic Play Area. Add multicultural items to other areas, such as multicultural figures to the Block Area.

STANDARD 2 ~ Community/Civics

Through their explorations, play, and social interactions, children demonstrate an understanding of what it means to be a participating member of groups and communities.

Benchmarks

By the end of their preschool years, most children will

1. Demonstrate confidence in expressing individual opinions and thoughts

2. Demonstrate respect for the thoughts and opinions of others, even when different from their own

3. Demonstrate understanding that communities are composed of groups of people who live, play, or work together and identify communities to which they belong

4. Participate in creating and following rules and routines

5. Take responsibility for simple tasks that contribute to the well-being of the group

Promoting Understanding of Community/Civics

Hold group meetings to talk about upcoming events, have project-related discussions, and discuss other matters that affect the group. Encourage children to express their own opinions and contribute to group discussions and decisions, while respecting the right of others to hold different views.

Include children in helping with jobs around the room. Rotate tasks among the children so everyone can feel they are a participating member of the group and learn responsibility. Involve everyone in cleanup time and use a cleanup song or other favorite song to make the work more enjoyable.

Involve children in making simple rules for the classroom or group. Talk about reasons for having rules, including making sure everyone feels safe and knows what is expected of them. Ask children to develop rules with you.

Our Rules

Be nice to each other.

Respect other people's things.

Tell the truth.

Be careful and safe.

Invite children to think about something they can do to help others. If there is a disaster they are seeing and hearing about on the news, such as a flood or fire, you might suggest doing something together that may help, such as collecting used books or toys. Children could also contribute to their families or communities by making cards or artwork for grandparents or the elderly in a neighborhood nursing home.

STANDARD 3 ~ History/Time

Through their explorations, play, and social interactions, children demonstrate an understanding of the passage of time and how the past influences their future.

Benchmarks

By the end of their preschool years, most children will

1. Describe past, current, and future events

2. Describe their day and upcoming activities in terms of daily routines ("First we . . . , then we . . . ")

3. Describe how a past event relates to something happening currently or in the future

4. Share stories or pictures about themselves in the past

Promoting Understanding of History/Time

Take photos at the beginning, middle, and end of field visits and other special occasions. Lay the photos out on the table and encourage children to put the pictures in order. Other pictures can document beginning, middle, and end-of-year events to arrange according to their occurrence. These photos can also be hung on the wall and referred to throughout the year.

Display a photo or picture of an upcoming event, along with numbers to count down days to the event. Cross off one number each day as the time draws closer.

Post a picture or photo schedule of daily activities that children can refer to throughout the day. Add interest to the schedule by including pictures related to your project or theme.

Make personal histories of each child, using photographs or drawings of the children as infants, as toddlers, and as they look now. Talk with children about how they have grown and the skills they have acquired as a result of their past efforts and experiences.

Engage children in discussions to foster their sense of time. Ask them to describe experiences they have had. Talk about events and activities of the day. Use words such as *yesterday, today, tomorrow, past, present,* and *future*.

STANDARD 4 ~ Geography/Places, People, and Environments

Through their explorations, play, and social interactions, children demonstrate an awareness of their physical environment and its impact on daily living.

Benchmarks

By the end of their preschool years, most children will

1. Describe where they live and where others live in relationship to them

2. Identify various living environments, such as farm, ranch, city, town, and country

3. Describe familiar places in their environment, such as a house, classroom, park, lake, or river

4. Draw or build representations of familiar places with a variety of materials

5. Identify various weather conditions and seasons and how they affect what we wear and what we do

6. Name natural resources, such as water, soil, clean air, and trees, and describe how they help us and how we can be good stewards of the environment

Promoting Understanding of Geography/Places, People, and Environments

The Block Area is an excellent place for children to learn simple geography terms and concepts, including *over, under, up, down, near,* and *far.* They can also learn them in a gross motor area or outside, where they can make these movements with their bodies.

In the Library Area, children can look at picture books about different places and geographic features, such as deserts, mountains, and rivers. Read books about various geographic places and point out items to help build children's vocabularies, including *bridge, hill, woods, lake,* and *road.* Display posters of different geographic places. Use photo albums or homemade books to exhibit postcards or pictures from around the country or around the world.

Take photographs of the neighborhood to share with the children. This allows you to bring the neighborhood to them if they aren't able to experience it firsthand. Make a book about the neighborhood using these pictures. Children can dictate sentences to write under the pictures. Use construction paper, tagboard, or photo albums to make these books. Make a simple map of the neighborhood to include in the book. Locate major buildings and homes on the map.

Take walks around the neighborhood, if possible, to look at buildings, schools, parks, playgrounds, or other places of interest. Observe different types of homes and/or apartments in the neighborhood. Go to a construction site, if possible, to observe workers building a house or other structure. Provide materials, including clay, blocks, wood, paint, paper, and recycled materials, for children to make their own representations of what they observed. After visiting the neighborhood or a building under construction, come back to the room and help children assemble a Dramatic Play Area, representing what they've observed during the field visit. This might include a market, restaurant, bakery, post office, library, or a variety of shops.

Spend time outside during each of the seasons, if practical, and discuss the effects of the outside climate on the kinds of activities we are able to do and what we need to wear. Point out natural resources while outside or when reading informational books. Talk about why we need clean air and water, trees, and soil and what we can do to protect these resources. Suggest simple measures, such as turning off the water while brushing teeth and respecting nature by not littering and not removing growing things from their environment.

STANDARD 5 ~ Economics

Through their explorations, play, and social interactions, children demonstrate an understanding of how people work together to grow, produce, distribute, and consume goods and services that meet their wants and needs.

Benchmarks

By the end of their preschool years, most children will

1. Identify several community helpers and the services they provide

2. Describe source of familiar foods, such as milk, apples, and eggs

3. Express knowledge that money can be used to purchase goods

4. Demonstrate understanding that people work to earn money to provide for their families and buy what they need

Promoting Understanding of Economics

Introduce children to community helpers by reading books about various people in the community and the contributions they make. Invite community helpers to share their roles and experiences with the children by visiting your room. Follow this by visiting some of them where they work, if possible. There are a variety of hands-on materials related to community helpers that children can use in their play, such as puzzles, puppets, and toy figures. Adding clothing to the Dramatic Play Area similar to that worn by community helpers will allow children to further explore these roles.

Plan a visit to a store in your community. In preparation for the visit, talk with children about what kinds of goods the store might provide, what you might be able to purchase, and how much it would cost.

Make a chart or book with the children of things families need. Talk about how families earn money to purchase items they need. Make

TRY THIS!

Make butter from cream and talk about the fact that milk and cream come from cows.

Directions for Making Butter

Help children pour heavy whipping cream and a dash of salt into a small container with a tight-fitting lid. Make sure that it is no more than two-thirds full. Add a clean marble to speed the process if desired. Have children take turns shaking the container. You can mark each child's turn by singing a verse of a favorite song or counting to 10 in both English and another language. This can take up to 30 minutes of shaking, so allow children to work on other activities as the butter is passed around. Spread the butter on crackers or bread for all to enjoy!

another chart or book about work people do to earn money for their families. Invite family members to come in to talk about their jobs.

With the children's help, turn the Dramatic Play Area into a farm. Include farm clothing, plastic farm animals, tools, and vehicles. Ask children to think about what would be needed to make the farm successful and to paint their ideas on a mural that could provide the backdrop for the area. Read books about food and farming. Visit a farm, if possible, so children can see firsthand where some of our food comes from.

Supporting Children Who Are Bilingual Learners

Provide experiences throughout the day to help children who are learning new languages.

• Read simple books to small groups and individuals that will help them learn social studies concepts, as well as new words they can use. Include books with pictures that have labels in both English and other languages, such as *My Day/Mi Día,* by Rebecca Emberley. Other books that include pictures and words about homes, families, and grandparents are good choices. Share books that respectfully and authentically depict the cultures of the children in the group. Shen's Books (http://www.shens.com) is a good resource for multicultural books.

• Encourage children to tell stories about their families. Write their words as they speak and read the story back to them. This can be done in their home languages first, if you, a parent, older student, or volunteer can do this, and then translated into English.

• Help children record themselves telling a story or describing something they've learned. Play the tape back as you write it out with children.

• Change the Dramatic Play Area to correspond with the topic the children are studying and label objects in the area in the languages of the children. This will help you and the children learn each other's languages and lets families know their home languages are honored and respected.

• Invite family members to share stories with the children and encourage children to use storytelling as well.

• Learn key words and phrases in the children's languages so you can communicate basic messages with them.

Working With Children's Individual Needs

All children can learn social studies concepts at their own personal levels of development. Some adaptations or modifications may help children be more successful. Many of these suggestions will be helpful for all children in our programs:

• Give children ample time needed to express themselves and their opinions.
• Ask children to complete jobs around the room with a partner.
• Make sure the environment and materials involved in the social studies projects are physically accessible to all children.

- Make sure books, posters, and dolls in the room include children with a variety of abilities. These could include children in wheelchairs or wearing glasses, braces, or other assistive devices.
- Provide individual picture schedules of daily routines for children who may benefit from them.
- Make sure all children are able to fully participate in neighborhood and community trips. Visit sites ahead of time to become aware of any adaptations that may be needed for individual children.

Summary

Standards in social studies include the areas of Families/Cultures; Community/Civics; History/Time; Geography/Places, People, and Environment; and Economics. Projects and themes on social studies topics provide children with meaningful ways to learn social studies concepts, as well as knowledge and skills in all other areas of the curriculum. Families, homes, community, or stores are good topics for focused studies for young children.

SOURCE: Photo by Jim Frost; used with permission.

6

Engaging Children in Meaningful Literacy

A very important component of any preschool curriculum is a strong, effective, early literacy program. It is important in these early years to help children develop positive attitudes toward reading and writing.

What Research and the Experts Tell Us
Literacy Development

The National Research Council report *Starting Out Right* (Burns, Griffin, & Snow, 1999) points out that children who start out well in reading and writing tend to continue to do well. Children who start out having trouble tend to continue to have trouble unless we intervene and make a difference. It is our responsibility to help children get a good start. Research also indicates that successful readers and writers in elementary school have the following characteristics in common:

1. They have *phonological awareness* (including the ability to hear and distinguish individual sounds in spoken words and the ability to rhyme).

2. They understand the *alphabetic principle* (the concept that the sounds of speech can be represented by one or more letters of the alphabet) and have letter-name knowledge.

3. They have good vocabularies, including good oral language comprehension and the ability to use words to express themselves.

4. They can comprehend or understand what they read.

5. They have good fluency.

6. They have interest and motivation to read for a variety of purposes.

SOURCE: Neuman & Dickinson (2001); Snow, Burns, & Griffin (1998).

Knowing the characteristics that help children read and write successfully provides us with areas to focus on in our work with children. We need to plan experiences that will help children acquire literacy skills, while making sure the materials and activities we provide motivate and encourage them to develop a love of books and reading. When children enjoy books, they spend more time looking at them and learn to read them more easily. If they feel successful at their first attempts, they will be more interested in continuing their efforts. Children need opportunities to be successful and feel good about themselves as beginning readers and writers. Standards and benchmarks give us the target skills children need to acquire to form a foundation for future competence in literacy.

Sample Early Learning Guidelines for Language and Literacy

Standard 1 ~ Reading

Through their explorations, play, and social interactions, children use skills and strategies to get meaning from print.

Standard 2 ~ Writing

Through their explorations, play, and social interactions, children use writing and drawing as means of communication.

Standard 3 ~ Listening and Phonological Awareness

Through their explorations, play, and social interactions, children listen, identify, and respond to environmental sounds, directions, and conversations and have phonological awareness.

Standard 4 ~ Speaking/Communicating and Oral Language Development

Through their explorations, play, and social interactions, children successfully communicate for multiple purposes.

Standard 5 ~ Learning New Languages

Through their explorations, play, and social interactions, children demonstrate an understanding that there are multiple languages and begin to communicate in a language other than their home languages.

Engaging Children in Meaningful Literacy Through Projects

Literacy learning can be especially effective in the context of the Project Approach. By exploring a project topic, children may have the motivation to read books and write, learning letters and words as they use them in meaningful ways. They can develop rich vocabularies, surrounded by experiences related to the topic. Choose books to read to the children that will add to their understanding of the project topic and add books to the classroom library on the topic. While planning a visit to a field site to learn more about a topic, ask children to help you make a list of things they might see and then review what was seen on their return. Write a story with the children about the field visit, asking children to dictate what they learned and found interesting. Record their words and then read them back, pointing to the words as they are read. Pictures taken on the trip can be made into a book, with children dictating captions to write under each picture. The children can help you write thank-you notes, which all the children can sign, after a field visit, visitor, or other project-related experience.

A project might begin as you notice children's interest in a new store that has moved into the area or frequent conversations, such as that between Reindl and Lilliana, about going to stores with their families:

> "Sometimes we go to the grocery store. They have lots of foods I like. But not the vegetables I like."

> "Yeah, and sometimes we go to 'Two Loons' to get ice cream!"

You could respond to their interests by asking, "Would you like to learn more about stores? What kinds of stores would you like to investigate?" To begin the project, you could make a web with the children of all the different topic areas they can think of related to stores. On another large sheet of paper, write down their comments about what they already know about stores and then what questions they have about them. Read back what you have written to help children make the connection between their spoken words and the words you have written. This process can be done inside or outdoors.

Include books about stores in the Library Area. Involve children in transforming the Dramatic Play Area into a store. They can help make signs for the store and use a toy cash register and play money to purchase items. They can sort and classify items to be sold on shelves and take on a variety of roles, such as shopkeeper, salesperson, baker, waitress, or customer. This project could last for several weeks or could be extended as long as children's interest remains. The topic could branch out into related fields and new opportunities for learning literacy as children's interests and questions lead them.

Designing the Environment

The design of our environment can help children reach standards and benchmarks. Children can be learning literacy throughout the day as they play in a variety of interest areas.

Library/Reading Area

Create a cozy Reading Area where children can develop a love of books and reading. This area would include the following:

- Children's books
  - fiction and informational books
  - books that reflect diverse cultures, especially the cultures of the children in the program
  - alphabet books
  - rhyming books

- ○ poetry
- ○ wordless books

- Books made by the children
- Books on tape or CD
- Children's magazines
- Flannel boards with story characters
- Washable pillows and beanbag chairs
- Puppets and washable stuffed animals
- Green plants and flowers

Writing Area

The way we prepare the environment can promote children's writing development. We can create a Writing Area with the following materials:

- Various types of paper
- Writing tablets
- Crayons
- Pencils
- Washable markers
- Alphabet chart or poster to provide a model of the letters

Additional Literacy Areas

Set up additional areas where children can choose to play with letters and words. Provide hands-on literacy materials on low shelves, tables, or mats on the floor that children can readily access. Include the following materials:

- Magnetic letters
- Alphabet blocks
- Alphabet and word puzzles
- Large alphabet beads for stringing

The entire environment can promote literacy. Having meaningful print around the room at the children's level allows them to begin to make connections between print and the message it conveys (International Reading Association [IRA] & National Association for the Education of Young Children [NAEYC], 1998). All areas of the room can be enhanced to become literacy areas by adding books, magazines, notebooks, and pencils. Other ways to add meaningful print to the room include the following:

- Post a schedule with the daily routine using words and symbols to represent activities.
- Label shelves with pictures and names of toys/materials that are stored there.
- Hang posters with words to favorite poems and fingerplays.

Addressing Standards Through Engaging Experiences and Activities

The remainder of this chapter provides sample standards and benchmarks for literacy and activities to help children reach them. These suggestions could be used in the context of a long-term project or theme or used individually. Knowing children's individual levels of development will allow adults to intentionally plan appropriate, engaging experiences that will help preschool children at all levels make progress in their understanding of literacy concepts.

STANDARD 1 ~ Reading

Through their explorations, play, and social interactions, children use skills and strategies to get meaning from print.

Benchmarks

By the end of their preschool years, most children will

1. Demonstrate motivation, interest, and enjoyment in books, reading, and acting out stories while engaged in play
2. Demonstrate book-handling skills, such as holding a book right-side up and turning pages from front to back
3. Recognize familiar environmental print, such as "STOP" signs, and realize it has meaning
4. Retell a story from a familiar book and relate it to real-life experiences
5. Make predictions of next steps in a story
6. Demonstrate knowledge that a symbol can represent something else (e.g., a word can stand for an object, a name for a person, a picture for the real object)

7. Recognize own first name in print

8. Demonstrate knowledge of the alphabetic principle, the concept that the sounds of speech can be represented by one or more letters of the alphabet

9. Identify at least 10 letters of the alphabet, especially those in their own names

10. Demonstrate knowledge of the basic concepts of print, such as knowing the differences between pictures, letters, and words

Promoting Reading

Reading to children has been found to be one of the most effective ways for children to learn how to read. Make it a priority to read to children many times throughout the day. This can include reading to the following:

- The whole group
- Small groups
- Individuals

Each reading experience should be fun and enjoyable for the children. The more they enjoy it, the more they will want to repeat it, allowing their literacy skills to improve. Make sure the books reflect children's interests and cultures and present positive role models of both men and women. Children enjoy hearing favorite stories again and again; and brain research confirms that repetition helps form connections in the brain. Use big books when reading to the whole group, if possible. Big books provide a *shared lap experience* and allow all children to see the words.

Tips for Reading to Children

- Use puppets, flannel board characters, and other props that relate to the story to capture children's interest and attention.
- Ask children to predict what a story might be about after showing them the cover of a book. Periodically, ask what might happen next in the story as you read.
- Help children learn letters and sounds in a meaningful way by pointing out key letters in the title of books you read.
- As you read, identify the "beginning" and "end" of books.
- Run your finger under words as you read them to help children learn that reading proceeds from left to right.
- Encourage children to join in reading simple, predictable books that have only a few words on each page, such as *It Looked Like Spilt Milk*, to promote fluency. Children can also repeat these predictable lines as they act out favorite stories.
- Ask *who, what, when, where*, and *why* questions to increase children's comprehension skills.
- Describe new and interesting words found in books to build children's vocabularies.
- Include poetry, fingerplays, and songs to keep children actively involved.

Working with children's names is a very effective way for them to learn literacy. Children's names are very meaningful to them, and they can learn a great deal by working with that special word. Children's cubbies or personal spaces where jackets or individual supplies are stored can be labeled with their names and photos. Encourage children to write their names on each piece of artwork they do and use this art to decorate the room.

Music is a powerful way for children to learn literacy. Provide books with familiar songs, like "The Wheels on the Bus" and "Twinkle, Twinkle Little Star," and sing them frequently with the children. Write other songs, such as "The ABC Song" and "Row, Row, Row Your Boat" on chart paper and point to the words as you sing.

Involve families by creating a lending library of books children can take home to read. These can be very easy books with just a few words on the page and pictures that help tell the story. Books that you have read repeatedly are especially good because children will be familiar with them and can begin to read them on their own. Encourage families to visit the public library. They not only have books to borrow but also often have tapes, CDs, or even toys you and your children's families can use.

STANDARD 2 ~ Writing

Through their explorations, play, and social interactions, children use writing and drawing as means of communication.

Benchmarks

By the end of their preschool years, most children will

1. Demonstrate motivation to draw and write during play, experimenting with writing tools, such as pencils, crayons, markers, and the computer keyboard

2. Demonstrate understanding that their spoken words can be represented with written letters or symbols as they dictate

3. Use scribbling and drawing to represent their ideas, and then begin to use letters and developmental or invented spelling of words to communicate messages

4. Attempt to write their own names using a variety of materials

5. Use environmental print (such as signs, labels on food, and general print around them) to help in their writing and ask adults for help in writing messages, lists, and stories.

Promoting Writing

Add writing materials to interest areas around the room to encourage children's writing:

- *Writing Area:* Add an old typewriter and rubber stamps with washable inkpads.
- *Dramatic Play Area:* Introduce small notepads and pencils for notes, letters, and grocery lists.
- *Block Area:* Supply cardstock or heavy paper and washable markers to encourage children to make signs for their constructions.

- *Science Area:* Include clipboards or notebooks for children to record observations of plant growth, cloud formations, baby animals' development, or sink-and-float experiments.
- *Math Area:* Provide chalk and small chalkboards or whiteboards with markers.
- *Computer Area:* Choose developmentally appropriate software for children to use if a computer is available. The computer area can be a rich source of writing possibilities. Children can use word-processing programs, such as Microsoft Word, if we enlarge the font so they can read it more clearly. They can also use writing software designed for children. We can type for them as they dictate to us and turn more of the control over to them as their skills progress. Most children will be able to at least type their names on the computer if given the opportunity.
- *Art Area:* Stock this area with a variety of art and writing supplies. The Art Area offers rich potential for writing. Ask children to dictate a short description or story about their art that can be included on another piece of paper and attached to their work.

TRY THIS!

> Provide fun writing tools for children to use. Pencils could be decorated to correspond with the topic being studied by attaching a leaf, artificial flower, sticker, or even a small plastic animal to the pencil top.

Children learn how to read and write better if they have experiences with both reading and writing at the same time. Reading and writing support each other. The skills learned in one area strengthen and support the other. As children begin to write, they begin to understand that the written word is made up of letters and sounds and that the words can convey meaning. This understanding is critical to both the reading and writing processes.

The writing process begins with children scribbling and drawing. With many opportunities to try out their skills, they will progress through several stages of writing. Older preschool children may try writing words on their own. Initially, their attempts will not be accurate, but we can invite them to try writing the letters they think are in the words they want to write. Recent research has shown that these attempts at invented or estimated spelling will help children become successful readers and writers (Sipe, 2001). Encouraging children's attempts at invented spelling will give them confidence to continue in their writing efforts. This early writing should not be "corrected," but celebrated with the child as an important step in the writing process.

Stages of Children's Writing

Drawing

Scribbling

Letterlike forms

Well-learned units/Letter strings

Invented spelling

Transitional

Conventional

SOURCE: Sulzby (1985)

Signing one's own name to something meaningful, such as a letter to a loved one, can be a real key to a child unlocking the literacy puzzle. As children learn to recognize their names in print, they are beginning to see that letters and words can stand for something else—themselves! As we sound out their names with them, they begin to see that each letter has a sound and that these sounds can be combined to form words. Encourage children to sign their names to all the art and writing they do to give them practice writing their names in meaningful contexts.

Provide areas where children can experiment with writing letters and words with a variety of materials. Spread a layer of shaving cream, salt, cornmeal, or other material on a tray, where children can use their fingers to write letters and words. Make play dough with the children and have it available on trays where children can form their names and other letters. Add alphabet cookie-cutters occasionally. A recipe for play dough can be found in Chapter 8, "Fostering Creativity Through the Arts."

Shared writing can be used to introduce children to the writing process. In shared writing, we gather small groups of children together and write on a large sheet of paper for the whole group to see. Writing topics can include current projects or themes, recent trips or visitors, or anything children are interested in. Ask children to share their thoughts on the topic as you write them. Every day offers new possibilities for these experiences. Make lists in which children contribute ideas on their favorite pets, colors, or things to do at a certain time of year:

Maria likes to . . .

Paulo likes to . . .

Reading these patterned lists together after writing them will also help improve children's blossoming reading skills.

Model writing at other times throughout the day by making lists, writing messages, and writing out words to songs and poems on large sheets of paper. Share your thoughts out loud as you write with the children, so they can understand the process you go through to write. Briefly mention letters and words you are writing and note when you are beginning and ending sentences. This process should be used only for short periods of time to keep it interesting for the children. Try to demonstrate your own enjoyment, interest, and motivation to write, showing children that writing is fun and useful.

Give children opportunities to dictate letters and stories to help them learn to write. Invite a child to dictate a letter to a family member or friend or describe a recent event. As the child speaks, write down word-for-word what is said. "Think aloud" as you write the words, sounding out words and pointing out when you are finishing a sentence or starting a new one. When the child finishes dictating, a critical step in the process is reading the work back to the child and moving your finger under each word as you say it. A short letter or story with only a few sentences is ideal. This process allows children to see that spoken words can be written and that print carries a message.

Making books with children is a great way for them to understand what an author does as they experience being authors themselves. Stapling a few sheets of paper together with construction paper covers is a simple way to make books. Allow children to draw pictures and dictate a story on a topic of their choice. Provide children with plain paper or paper cut into a shape relating to a topic you are exploring. Staple the papers together, adding wallpaper or other heavy paper as a cover.

TRY THIS!

Help children write books on the computer. Ask them to think about a story and what could happen first, next, and at the end. Act as their scribe, typing their thoughts. Read their stories back to them. Children could choose graphics to add to their stories or do the illustrations themselves. Place these books in the Library Area, where the young author can read and share them with other children.

Bookmaking Ideas

- Make variations of favorite books, such as *Brown Bear, Brown Bear, What Do You See?* To go along with a farm project, each child could draw a picture of a farm animal. You can bind the pictures together and write phrases such as, "White cow, white cow, what do you see?" to accompany a child's picture of a cow and on the next page with a drawing of a pig write, "Pink pig, pink pig, what do you see?"

- Make books with photos of the children. This could be another version of *Brown Bear, Brown Bear* or simply include a photo of each child and his or her name. The book could contain color words or shapes, with a single, predictable phrase on each page, such as "Jamal likes *blue.*" Photo albums, cardboard, or construction paper can be used to make these books. Other simple, predictable books can also be made using photo albums.

- Make books with paper plates by stapling them together or punching holes and tying yarn through the holes. Covers of the paper plate books could be plates with designs already on them, or children could enjoy coloring the edges of white paper plates to make the covers.

- Ziplock bags make interesting books, too. Photos, leaves, and other items from nature or words from familiar cereal boxes can be placed in the bags and taped if necessary. Include file cards with words labeling the objects or telling a story. To bind the books, staple the bags together or punch holes in them and tie yarn through the holes.

STANDARD 3 ~ Listening and Phonological Awareness

Through their explorations, play, and social interactions, children listen, identify, and respond to environmental sounds, directions, and conversations and have phonological awareness.

Benchmarks

By the end of their preschool years, most children will

1. Listen and respond to conversations with adults and other children during play
2. Identify sounds and words in their daily environment
3. Listen attentively to books and stories
4. Repeat familiar songs, rhymes, and phrases from favorite storybooks
5. Demonstrate understanding of an increasingly rich vocabulary
6. Follow simple directions with two or more steps
7. Recognize some rhyming sounds
8. Demonstrate the ability to hear individual parts of words and separate the parts using clapping, finger snapping, or other movement (e.g., clapping out each syllable of "pup-py," "di-no-saur")
9. Identify words that begin with the same sound from a small group of words
10. Repeat spoken words when requested

Promoting Listening and Phonological Awareness

Children love listening to stories in a cozy corner, sitting on a lap, in a loft, or outside under a tree. Listening to stories helps children develop phonological awareness and listening skills, as well as increasing vocabulary, fluency, comprehension, and general knowledge. Equip a Listening Area with the following:

- Tape or CD player with headphones
- Adaptors for multiple headsets
- Books on tape or CD, available at your local library

Try making your own tapes for the Listening Area by recording yourself or other familiar voices reading a story. Be inventive about the sounds that indicate that it is time to turn a page by using a variety of musical instruments, a bell, whistle, clapping sounds, or whatever might have an association with the story. Children can be involved in taping the stories, repeating predictable lines from a story or making the turn-the-page signal. Parents may also enjoy taping stories for the classroom and involving their children in the process.

Reading to children will increase their vocabularies and listening skills. Read a variety of culturally diverse books, poems, and nursery rhymes with children. Plan to read to children several times a day, both in small groups and individually. Take on different voices for characters. Change the tone and volume of your voice to capture and maintain children's interest. When older children are asked who they remember reading to them, they often recall someone who made the

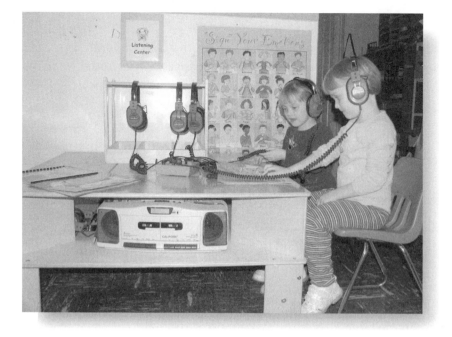

reading come alive by the voices and expression they used. To increase phonological awareness, point out rhyming words in a story like *Cat in the Hat.* Encourage children to also think of words that rhyme with keywords in a story or title.

Play a variety of interesting songs and music to increase children's listening skills and phonological awareness. Use children's songs and music from a variety of cultures. Sing songs with rhymes, including those that use children's names, such as "Wiloughby, Wallaby, Woo." Sing, for example, "Wiloughby, Wallaby, Wora, an elephant sat on Nora; Wiloughby, Wallaby, Wiego, an elephant sat on Diego." You may also want to provide musical instruments that children can use to play in rhythm with the individual sounds in the songs. This will help them distinguish the individual sounds in words, which is necessary for phonological awareness.

Play games to increase listening skills and phonological awareness. Involve children in games in which they listen and guess who or what is making a sound they are hearing. These can be sounds from objects found in the room or environmental sounds that have been taped from a variety of sources. Play clapping games in which children clap while saying or singing words, such as their names. Clapping as each individual syllable is said will help children be able to hear and identify separate sounds/syllables in words. Make a game of trying to find words that rhyme or start with the same sound.

STANDARD 4 ~ Speaking/Communicating and Oral Language Development

Through their explorations, play, and social interactions, children successfully communicate for multiple purposes.

Benchmarks

By the end of their preschool years, most children will

1. Play with the sounds of language, repeating rhymes, songs, poems, and fingerplays

2. Use an increasingly rich vocabulary

3. Demonstrate motivation to communicate in play and everyday activities

4. Provide meaningful responses to questions and pose questions to learn new information or clarify ideas

5. Use complete sentences of varying length to express ideas and feelings through spoken language, sign language, or other forms of communication

6. Initiate and engage in conversation and discussions with adults and other children

7. Tell real or imaginary stories that have a recognizable beginning, middle, and end

What Research and the Experts Tell Us

Learning Language

Vygotsky wrote of the importance of language for all other learning. He described language as a *tool of the mind*, the most important of all the tools we use for learning. Language helps all other areas develop. Children need language in order to have words to describe concepts they are learning. Vygotsky believed children learn language in a social context, interacting, and communicating with other children and adults (Berk & Winsler, 1995; Bodrova & Leong, 1996).

Promoting Speaking/Communicating and Oral Language Development

Interest areas give children the opportunity to grow in their oral language development. Their vocabularies grow as they interact with toys, materials, and other children and adults in these areas. Hands-on science and math activities give children the opportunity to ask questions and learn new words. After children have finished working in the interest areas, provide time for them to talk about and share what they were involved in doing.

Change the props in the Dramatic Play Area to go along with a theme, project, or topic you are studying. Playing in the redesigned area will give children a reason to talk and use language. The new props provide opportunities for vocabulary development, as children interact with the fresh materials. For example, change the Dramatic Play Area into a shoe store, where children can talk about the shoes, slippers, and other materials they are playing

TRY THIS!

Set up a flower shop with silk flowers, plastic flowerpots, toy cash register, work gloves, watering can, and plastic garden tools. The shop could be located in the Sand Area, Housekeeping Area, or any area inside or outside. Have sand and/or potting soil available. Include books, such as **Planting a Rainbow**. Encourage children to fill containers, make flower arrangements, and talk with each other as they play.

with. Join in their play occasionally and make use of interesting words to expand their vocabularies.

Reading quality fiction and informational books to children is one of the best ways to help increase their vocabularies. Explain the meaning of unfamiliar words in the stories. Repeated readings of favorite books and having children join in reading predictable phrases will reinforce their acquisition of new words. Encourage children to retell and act out stories you have read together. Provide props, such as puppets, flannel board characters, and stuffed animals for them to use in their retellings. Ask questions about books and stories to give children the opportunity to practice using new words found in the story.

Take time to engage in rich conversations with children. Listen attentively, follow their lead, and allow them ample time to form their thoughts and sentences. Expand on children's language; when a child says, "white dog," respond with "Yes, that is a pretty, little, white dog." Talk about your own actions as you interact with the child, describing out loud what you are doing and thinking. Provide opportunities for children to talk with each other in interest areas, during snack and lunch times, and in informal conversations, both inside and outside.

Fill the day with music and singing! Singing is an excellent way to promote children's speaking and oral language development. Sing favorite songs to begin and end the day. Play children's songs on CDs or tapes while they are playing in interest areas, including songs from various cultures. Encourage children to play with the sounds of the words found in the songs by repeating or changing the beginning sounds.

Take trips around the neighborhood or even in your own building, so that children are exposed to new people, places, and things. Talk about the new surroundings and objects, using descriptive words, and encourage discussion about them as well. Visit places related to the current project of study, giving children new experiences and concepts to talk about.

STANDARD 5 ~ Learning New Languages

Through their explorations, play, and social interactions, children demonstrate an understanding that there are multiple languages and begin to communicate in a language other than their home languages.

Benchmarks

By the end of their preschool years, most children will

1. Name at least one example of a language other than their home languages

2. Say simple greetings in another language, such as *"hola"* ("hello" in Spanish) and *"adiós"* ("good-bye" in Spanish) or use sign language to express a greeting

For a child learning English as a new language:

3. Listen to peers and adults speaking in English to learn new information, and show some understanding of the language

4. Engage in nonverbal communication with those who speak a language other than their native languages

5. Play with the sounds and intonation of the English language as well as their home languages

6. Identify names of common objects in the environment

7. Use simple words and phrases to communicate with adults and other children

When teaching a new language to children who already know English, use a language that is most appropriate for your children and community. If many people in the community speak Spanish, this would be a natural choice.

What Research and the Experts Tell Us

Learning a New Language

Brain research has shown that the early years are the best time to learn a foreign language. Children need to hear the sounds of a language early in order to speak like a native later on. Playing CDs or tapes of music in other languages and teaching simple words will help children form a foundation for the languages they hear (Shore, 1997).

Promoting Learning New Languages

Invite parents and members of the community who speak other languages to come in and teach children greetings and simple songs. Invite them to teach children simple games they remember from childhood, along with a few key words used in the games.

Teach color words in another language by pointing out the colors of children's clothes and the colors of items in the room. Ask children to find items as you call out a color, such as purple *(purpúreo)* or white *(blanco)*. Teach children to count in another language and provide daily opportunities for them to count using these numbers.

Teach children words associated with topics they are exploring. This helps children learn words associated with the topic in context, and therefore they are more likely to understand and remember the new words. For children learning English as a new language, these could be English words connected to the topic. For children who already speak English, they could be learning words related to the project in other languages. Projects on families, cultures, homes, or languages would be excellent topics for learning new languages, but any topic offers potential.

English	Spanish
family	*familia*
house	*casa*
mother	*madre*
father	*padre*
brother	*hermano*
sister	*hermana*
tree	*arbor*

water	*agua*
bird	*ave*
green	*verde*
blue	*azul*
red	*rojo*
orange	*naranja*
yellow	*amarillo*

Sing to the tune of "London Bridge."

Autumn leaves are falling down, falling down, falling down,
Autumn leaves are falling down, red, orange, yellow,
Rojo, naranja, amarillo

This song could be repeated throughout the autumn to help children learn color words. You could ask children to help you compose new words each season or to go along with a project, topic, or theme.

TRY THIS!

Sing "It's a Small World" in other languages, such as Spanish:

Es [It's] un mundo [a world] muy pequeño [very small].
Es un mundo muy pequeño.
Es un mundo muy pequeño.
Es un pequeño, pequeño mundo.

Use motions to go along with the song to help children learn the words.

Dolls and puppets provide opportunities for children to use language. In her book *The Anti-Biased Curriculum: Tools for Empowering Young Children* (1989), Louise Derman-Sparks and the ABC Task Force have recommended using *persona dolls*, each of which has its own culture and life story, to help children connect with and respect people from diverse backgrounds. In a similar way, we can assign dolls or puppets specific languages that they will use whenever they "speak." One doll may speak only Spanish, while another doll speaks Chinese, and another Tagalog. We can speak for the dolls whose languages we know and ask family members, older students, or volunteers who speak additional languages to be the voices for others. Encourage the children to use the dolls' or puppets' languages when playing with them.

Introduce new languages through books and music. Find books that are available in more than one language. Books such as *Goodnight Moon (Buenas Noches Luna)* and *Where the Wild Things Are (Donde Viven los Monstruos)*, available in both English and Spanish, are simple to read and can help children to see the connection between the two languages. There are also a number of simple picture dictionaries and books, such as *Dora's Book of Words (Libro de Palabras de Dora)*, that provide words in both English and another language. After sharing these with the children, provide copies in the Library Area. Add books and songs on tapes or CDs in multiple languages to the Listening Area. Sing simple songs in other languages, such as "Frère Jacques" in French. Teach children simple songs in sign language.

Names are very meaningful to young children. Use another language to ask children to tell you their names. *"¿Cómo te llamas?"* (in Spanish).

Children would respond *"Me llamo _____."* Teach children a simple greeting, such as *"Hola"* ("hello" in Spanish). Then use this greeting with the children in the morning. Encourage them to greet you and the other children the same way. Children could also use their names in greetings such as the following:

"How are you, Cody?" *"¿Cómo estás, Cody?"*

And responses could include the following:

Spanish	English
excelente	excellent
muy bien	very good
bien	good
mal	not good
¿y tú?	and you?

Supporting Children Who Are Bilingual Learners

Creating an environment where children feel respected and know that they can experiment and make mistakes will enhance their ability to learn a new language. Children also need many opportunities to talk and play with each other and learn language in meaningful ways.

What Research and the Experts Tell Us

Learning English as a New Language

"The desire to communicate is at the heart of young children's second language learning" (Vukelich, Christie, & Enz, 2002, p. 37). A family needs to know that their home language is respected and that they should continue to communicate with their children in that language. The second language adds to the child's repertoire and should not replace it.

Being able to speak two languages is an asset to children (NAEYC, 1995). A child's first language forms the foundation for learning a new language. Many professionals suggest that we help children learn about books, print, and phonological awareness initially in the language in which they feel most competent. Children will learn the new skills and then be able to transfer them to English as they become more proficient. Children benefit from hearing both languages spoken and hearing books read in both languages. They also need to feel comfortable before they are able to speak a new language. This will happen best in a safe, reassuring environment where children know they do not need to talk until they feel willing to do so. Children need plenty of time to respond without feeling rushed and benefit from activities they can participate in for a while without having to speak, such as table toys, blocks, and puzzles (Meier, 2004; NAEYC, 1995; Vukelich et al., 2002).

There are many things we can do to help children who are learning English as a second language or who are learning their families' native languages.

- Learn a few key words and phrases in the children's native languages so you can communicate important needs and concepts. Teach basic words in these languages to all children in the program so they can communicate with each other. If possible, have an aide or volunteer in the room who speaks the child's native language.
- Use simple sentences, words that are easily understood, and words that will help the child meet his or her needs. Point to objects as you refer to them and use gestures and facial expressions.
- Speak slowly and model language use, occasionally emphasizing beginning and ending sounds.
- When speaking with children, build on their attempts at using the new language by using correct vocabulary and format in a conversational style, rather than correcting the children.
- Have books available both in English and in the children's native languages. It is also good to have a selection of books that reflect the children's cultures.
- Write class books about children's families, homes, meals, celebrations, pets, and other aspects of their lives.
- Display signs and label objects around the room in the children's home languages, as well as English. Use different colors for each language.
- Provide a listening center with stories and songs on tape in children's native languages, as well as English.
- Encourage children to talk with each other. Ask a child who speaks English well to be a buddy to a child learning English. Provide suggestions to the buddy about how he or she can play, talk with, and support the child learning the language.
- Use songs to help children learn new words and phrases, such as a "Hello, how are you?" song.

Working With Families

- Involve families in the program. Children will feel more secure if they know their parents are involved. Encourage parents to continue to speak to their children in their native languages at home.
- Have books in multiple languages for children to take home to read with their families. Bess Press (http://www.besspress.com), Libros Sin Fronteras (http://www .librossinfronteras.com), China Sprout (http://www.chinasprout.com), and the American Library Association (http://www.alastore.ala.org) are a few of the publishing organizations that offer quality bilingual books and books in other languages.
- Invite parents, volunteers, and older children who speak the child's language to make audiotapes of stories in the child's language.

Working With Children's Individual Needs

All children benefit from good teaching practices, including working in interest areas and listening to books being read. For children who have special needs, there are several additional things we can do to help them reach the standards. Many of these suggestions will be helpful for all children in our programs:

- Plan time in the day to work with individuals and small groups.
- Teach children a few basic words in sign language and use them with familiar songs and phrases to provide another means of communication.
- Use interactive books that allow children to be more involved in the process by pressing buttons.
- Provide board books with sturdy cardboard pages on shelves where children can easily reach them.
- For children who have difficulty turning pages, purchase or make page-turning devices and book stands to hold books in place.
- Provide books with large print for children who have difficulty with vision. Organizations, such as the American Council for the Blind and the Braille Institute of America, will donate special equipment for these children to use as well.
- Use many concrete, hands-on visual materials when helping children learn new words.
- Allow children to take turns holding a special wand or other interesting item that indicates that it is their turn to speak. Give children plenty of time to respond to questions.
- Provide oversized pencils, crayons, and markers or rubber pencil grips that fit over pencils to make them easier to grasp.
- Offer a variety of paper, including heavier paper and even sandpaper, to help children who are having difficulty writing. Providing a slanted surface by using a large binder, or writing on easels or large paper taped to the wall can also be helpful.
- Use touch screens and interactive programs on the computer and augmented-communication devices for children who need them. There are adaptive keyboards and voice recognition software programs that make it easier for children to work on the computer.
- Take photos of the children performing routine activities of the day and post these on a board to help those who have difficulty understanding directions.
- Provide plastic toy phones (which can be made from plastic PVC pipes and corners) that allow children to hear themselves speak, providing immediate feedback. This is especially helpful for children who need additional help with speech and language.
- Use songs and fingerplays between transitions. Keep in mind that each day is filled with teachable moments and opportunities for fun, enjoyable learning.

Summary

Literacy forms a foundation for learning in all other areas. As children progress in literacy, they learn words, concepts, and understandings that will help them develop in all other areas of the curriculum. Reading, writing, listening, phonological awareness, speaking, communicating, and oral language development are all critical components of literacy. It is important that we provide a rich language environment for all children, including those who are learning English as a new language and those who are learning their families' native languages. Brain research has shown that the preschool years are an optimal time for all children to be learning new languages. Projects and themes give children meaningful opportunities to learn literacy and new vocabulary associated with the topic. Participating in activities related to project topics and engaging with others in literacy-rich interest areas provide children with the tools they need to be successful in literacy.

7

Making Mathematics Inviting

hildren can gain a solid foundation for mathematics throughout the entire day as they play and participate in routine activities. As children build with blocks and string patterns with beads, they are learning concepts of geometry and algebra. They develop their number sense as they count out the number of cups they need to set the table for lunch. We need to build on children's previous experiences and help them understand that they already know much about mathematics. It is important for them to develop positive attitudes toward mathematics and self-confidence in their ability to solve problems. As children engage in interesting, hands-on activities, they can develop a real fascination with mathematics. The more opportunities children have to experience mathematics, the more their skills will develop.

What Research and the Experts Tell Us
Young Children and Mathematics

In their joint position statement on *Early Childhood Mathematics* (2002), the National Council of Teachers of Mathematics (NCTM) and the National Association for the Education of Young Children (NAEYC) have several recommendations for providing quality mathematics education for preschool children, including the following:

1. Provide time and materials for children to engage in play.

2. Enhance children's natural interest and curiosity in mathematics and their disposition to use it to make sense of their world.

3. Provide adult support, building on children's family, linguistic, and cultural backgrounds and experiences.

4. Encourage children's problem solving and reasoning through integrated activities.

5. Provide for sustained interaction with mathematical ideas; and continually assess children's mathematical knowledge and skills.

NCTM has developed standards in the areas of Number and Operations, Algebra, Geometry, Measurement, and Data Analysis and Probability. Knowing preschool standards and benchmarks for mathematics helps to guide our work with children and plan activities that will help them acquire the skills they need. Listed below are sample standards for preschool mathematics. Research has shown that children are capable of learning a great deal of mathematics during their preschool years. They are beginning to understand concepts of geometry when they work with *shapes.* They learn the foundations for algebra when they make *patterns,* and they even begin the foundation for statistics when they participate in making *graphs.* When adults know what skills are appropriate for children to be learning during these years, they can plan interesting experiences, with hands-on materials that will help them make progress in understanding these mathematical concepts.

Sample Early Learning Guidelines for Mathematics

STANDARD 1 ~ Number Sense and Operations

Through their explorations, play, and social interactions, children count with understanding and use numbers to tell how many, describe order, and compare.

STANDARD 2 ~ Shapes/Geometry

Through their explorations, play, and social interactions, children identify and describe simple geometric shapes (circle, triangle, rectangle) and show an awareness of their positions in relation to other objects.

STANDARD 3 ~ Measurement

Through their explorations, play, and social interactions, children identify and compare the attributes of length, volume, weight, time, and temperature and use the tools needed to measure them.

STANDARD 4 ~ Data Analysis and Probability

Through their explorations, play, and social interactions, children classify, organize, represent, and use information to ask and answer questions.

STANDARD 5 ~ Patterns/Algebra

Through their explorations, play, and social interactions, children identify, repeat, and describe simple patterns using concrete objects.

Making Mathematics Meaningful Through Projects

Children can learn a great deal about mathematical concepts as they explore projects. Projects give children meaningful opportunities to develop a sense of number. They can count objects they are studying and compare groups of objects related to the topic. Exploring projects can provide children with background knowledge that will help them be able to sort and classify. As children learn more about the topic, they gain a deeper understanding of the characteristics and properties of the objects involved in their study that will help them with classification. Projects provide children with meaningful contexts to learn how to make sense of data. Making graphs relating to topics they are exploring can help children make sense of the information they are learning (data analysis).

After observing children talking about motorcycles and bikes over an extended period of time, you might decide to do a project or focused study on transportation. You might hear conversations such as the following:

"I like to ride my motorcycle. I like to go for car rides on it. It's a bike motorcycle."

"Bikes are my favorite thing to do. I wish we could ride bikes all the time."

In a project on transportation, have children graph their favorite type of vehicle by gluing a picture of it on a large graph; this will help children learn the beginning concepts of data analysis. They could measure the length of various toy cars and trucks and make patterns with them. Making patterns is the foundation of algebra and the primary focus of algebra in the preschool years.

Children can be learning about geometry (shapes) as they help convert the Dramatic Play Area into a bus, car, train, subway, or plane. They could use a large appliance box or convert the entire area to look like the inside of the vehicle with seats, steering wheels, gauges, and other components. Rich discussions about the vehicles and the shapes found within them can help children gain a deeper understanding of mathematical concepts.

Designing the Environment

Post a large number line from 1 to 10 in the room and point to the numbers as you count throughout the day. This could include counting the number of boys and girls present each day, the number that prefer a certain kind of milk, and project- or theme-related counting experiences.

1	2	3	4	5	6	7	8	9	10

Set up a Math Area, where children can explore mathematical concepts. Stock the area with many different types of materials children can count: colorful cubes, counting bears, plastic dinosaurs, and keys. Include number puzzles, dice, cards, and dominoes that children can use in their play.

Many other interest areas can contribute to children's mathematical development. The Block Area is a wonderful place for children to learn geometry and other math skills through play. Wooden unit blocks are ideal for helping children learn basic concepts. As children build with the blocks, they can begin to recognize shapes and see how one shape is related to another. The Art Area also offers rich possibilities for children to learn more about math. Provide many different shapes and sizes of construction paper for children to use creatively in their art. Invite children to make three-dimensional shapes out of play dough and talk with them about the shapes they are making. As children play, we can talk with them about what they are doing and observing, promoting their mathematical thinking while being careful to support, not interrupt, their construction and creativity.

Provide a water table or large plastic container of water where children can play with measuring cups and containers of varying sizes. As children play, talk with them about which containers hold "more," "less," or "the same." Give children similar experiences with a sand table or container of sand. Remove the sand periodically and replace it with other sensory materials, such as aquarium rocks or pebbles, to keep interest levels high.

Addressing Standards Through Engaging Experiences and Activities

The remainder of this chapter will go more in depth with each standard, outlining benchmarks and providing suggestions to meet them through hands-on activities. These activities can be done in the context of a project or theme or used independently. Knowing children's current mathematical understanding will allow adults to intentionally plan appropriate, engaging experiences that will help preschool children at all levels make progress in their development of mathematical concepts.

STANDARD 1 ~ Number Sense and Operations

Through their explorations, play, and social interactions, children count with understanding and use numbers to tell how many, describe order, and compare.

Benchmarks

By the end of their preschool years, most children will

1. Count by one's to 10 and higher

2. Count the number of items in a group of up to 10 objects and know that the last number tells how many

3. Verbally count backward from five

4. Look at a group of up to four objects and quickly see and say the number of objects

5. Recognize and name numerals one to five

6. Compare two groups (containing up to five objects each) and describe them using comparative words, such as *more, less, fewer,* or *equal*

7. Use and understand the terms *first, last,* and *first* through *fifth*

8. Separate a collection of 10 items into two equal groups

9. Give up to five items when requested

Promoting Understanding of Number Sense and Operations

Use quality children's books and music to teach mathematics concepts. There are a number of appealing books, such as *Fish Eyes: A Book You Can Count On* and *One, Two, Three to the Zoo,* that introduce children to counting. There are also books with words to songs, such as *Five Little Ducks* and *Five Green and Speckled Frogs,* that children love to sing. Encouraging children to use their fingers as they sing these songs will help them learn to count both forward and backward. Write the words to songs, fingerplays, and number rhymes, such as "One, Two, Buckle My Shoe," on large chart paper. Repeat these often with the children, pointing to the words and numbers.

Ask children to point to numbers on the number line occasionally while counting. Pointing to the numbers while singing number songs will help children gain a deeper understanding. Ask children to take turns pointing to numbers on the number line while counting backward from 5. To make this more fun, children could stand on tiptoes when saying "five" and slowly move closer to the ground as each smaller number is said, ending by saying the number "one" while sitting on the floor. They could pretend to be taking off in a space shuttle and count down from 5. Once children are confident counting to 10 using the number line, extend the line to 20.

Take a number walk with children and encourage them to notice any numbers they see on street signs, houses, billboards, or yard signs. This could even be done inside. Use this opportunity to help children learn to count objects beginning with numbers other than the number one by saying things like, "We already saw two trees, now there are three, four, and five."

Talk with children as they play and occasionally help them count the objects they are using. Ask children to hand you different numbers of toys in their play: "Would you hand me four blocks we can add to this tower?" Have fun with the number zero. Ask children to hand you "zero blocks" or "zero puppies" or tell them you're going to give them "zero dinosaurs." Use the words *first, second, third, fourth,* and *fifth* to describe toys that are lined up. With the children, divide a few of the blocks or other toys you are playing with into two groups and ask them to help you compare the sets. Talk about the sets using words such as *more, less, equal,* and *the same as.*

STANDARD 2 ~ Shapes/Geometry

Through their explorations, play, and social interactions, children identify and describe simple geometric shapes (circle, triangle, rectangle) and show an awareness of their positions in relation to other objects.

Benchmarks

By the end of their preschool years, most children will

1. Recognize and name *circle, triangle,* and *rectangle* (which includes *square*)

2. Build and describe two-dimensional shapes, such as making circles and triangles with blocks and play dough

3. Recognize that a shape remains the same shape when it changes position

4. Sort and match objects with the same shape and size and lay an object of the same shape and size on top of another to show they are the same

5. Make a picture by combining shapes

6. Take a shape apart (decompose) to make new shapes, such as finding two triangles in a square

7. Demonstrate and begin to use the language of the relative position of objects in the environment and play situations, such as *up, down, over, under, top, bottom, inside, outside, in front, behind, between,* and *next to*

8. Create two-dimensional shapes and three-dimensional structures that have symmetry

Promoting Understanding of Geometry

Enhance the Block Area by adding toy animals and people and suggest that the children build homes for them. Then, ask the children to put the animals *beside, next to, behind, above, up, down, near,* and *far* from their homes, in order to help them understand these position words. Set out other types of blocks, such as waffle blocks or connecting blocks, for children to use in their constructions.

Provide opportunities for children to play with a variety of shapes. Talk with children as they play with the shapes, noticing how the shapes are alike and different. Point out that shapes remain the same even when turned upside down or sideways. Encourage children to combine shapes to make new ones, such as using two triangles to form a square. Then, ask them to take these and other combined shapes apart and talk about the shapes that remain. Set out three-dimensional objects, including cubes and pyramids; blocks or rods with graduated lengths, such as jumbo Cuisenaire Rods; and nesting cups. Set out trays in which children can sort toys or blocks according to size and shape. Draw simple outlines and ask children to fill them in with smaller shapes.

Integrate literacy and music by finding shapes in books such as *Color Zoo* and *Color Farm; Take Another Look; Shapes, Shapes, Shapes;* and *The Wheels on the Bus.* Play children's favorite music and ask them to hold hands, form a circle, and move to the music. Ask children to hold hands in groups of three and try to form a triangle, and groups of four to make a square. Vary this activity by giving children a long ribbon or piece of yarn to use as they make the shapes.

Play games of finding shapes in the environment, both indoors and outdoors. Provide clipboards and paper for the children to draw the shapes they see. Have fun with children pointing out examples of shapes, while also talking about why one object is a certain shape and another object isn't. "This section of the sidewalk has four equal sides and four equal corners; it's a square. This ball doesn't have four equal sides and four equal corners; it isn't a square."

Children can observe a neighborhood construction project, if one is under way, or look at buildings in the area. Help children take photographs of the buildings to display in the Block Area. They can then try to recreate models of the structures they observed with blocks, clay, play dough, or on paper.

Create an obstacle course in the room or outside. Ask children to describe their positions as they move through the course: *below* the table, *over* the chair, or *next to* the aquarium.

STANDARD 3 ~ Measurement

Through their explorations, play, and social interactions, children identify and compare the attributes of length, volume, weight, time, and temperature and use the tools needed to measure them.

Benchmarks

By the end of their preschool years, most children will

1. Compare length and other attributes of objects, using the terms *bigger, longer,* and *taller*

2. Compare two objects by placing one on top of another and indicate which object takes up more space

3. Arrange objects in order according to characteristics or attributes, such as height

4. Identify and use measurement tools, such as ruler, scales, measuring cups, thermometer, clock, and calendar

Promoting Understanding of Measurement

Children love to measure! Set out a variety of measuring devices in the Math Area, such as balance scales, safe thermometers, rulers, and measuring cups. Encourage children to measure and weigh a variety of objects, such as blocks or small plastic toys, with the measuring devices. Provide a variety of objects children can put in order according to size or length.

Plan cooking experiences with the children. Allow them to help measure and add ingredients. Write out recipes on large paper, including pictures of the ingredients, and point to the words as each item is added.

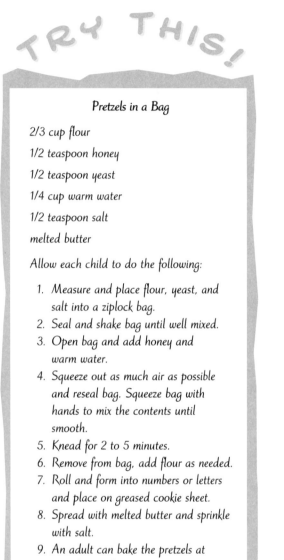

TRY THIS!

Pretzels in a Bag

2/3 cup flour

1/2 teaspoon honey

1/2 teaspoon yeast

1/4 cup warm water

1/2 teaspoon salt

melted butter

Allow each child to do the following:

1. Measure and place flour, yeast, and salt into a ziplock bag.
2. Seal and shake bag until well mixed.
3. Open bag and add honey and warm water.
4. Squeeze out as much air as possible and reseal bag. Squeeze bag with hands to mix the contents until smooth.
5. Knead for 2 to 5 minutes.
6. Remove from bag, add flour as needed.
7. Roll and form into numbers or letters and place on greased cookie sheet.
8. Spread with melted butter and sprinkle with salt.
9. An adult can bake the pretzels at 425 degrees for 12–20 minutes.
10. Let cool and enjoy.

Integrate literacy and music by reading stories such as *Is It Larger? Is It Smaller?; Inch by Inch;* and *Inch by Inch: The Garden Song.* In the Art Area, help children make their own inchworm measuring sticks by inviting them to draw inchworms on 1-inch pieces of tagboard. Help children glue 12 of their inchworms on a 12-inch strip of tagboard. Encourage children to use both their 1-inch inchworms and inchworm rulers to measure things around the room. Plastic inchworms for measuring are also available commercially. Sing the song "Inchworm" with the children as they measure.

Have fun measuring things around the room. Use many different standard and nonstandard tools to measure with, including rulers, blocks, or shoes. Plant seeds and help children measure the height of the plants each week and record the growth on a large chart. The measurements can be made with rulers, Unifix Cubes®, or other small blocks. Set a thermometer outside a window and observe the temperature each day. In the fall, bring in a pumpkin and ask children to estimate its circumference using a piece of yarn. Have children compare their yarn lengths to the actual pumpkin to check their estimations. Use a measuring tape to measure the pumpkin as well.

Measure each child's height at the beginning, middle, and end of the year. Record the measurements on a large chart so children can see their growth. Also measure their height with pieces of string and then compare the string lengths.

STANDARD 4 ~ Data Analysis and Probability

Through their explorations, play, and social interactions, children classify, organize, represent, and use information to ask and answer questions.

Benchmarks

By the end of their preschool years, most children will

1. Sort objects onto a large graph according to one attribute, such as size, shape, or color

2. Name the category that has the "most," "least," or "the same" on a large graph

3. Gather information to answer questions of interest

Promoting Understanding of Data Analysis and Probability

Provide a variety of objects with varying shapes, sizes, and textures. Supply interesting containers that children can use to sort the objects, such as baskets, muffin tins, and empty picture frames. As children sort, talk with them about their reasons for grouping certain objects together. Use items that reflect the children's cultures when possible, such as large, native beads.

Make a large graph on a sheet of paper. Children can sort items, such as wooden cubes, directly onto the graph, according to color or other attribute. Compare the columns with the children, talking about which has "more," "less," or "the same."

TRY THIS!

Make a large, reusable graphing mat by using an inexpensive white shower curtain and drawing vertical and horizontal lines. Do a graphing activity at least once a week with the children, using the graphing mat or large sheets of paper. Involve the children in collecting data for the graph by asking their peers questions such as their favorite foods, colors, or books. They could also gather data from their families by asking about favorite meals or songs.

STANDARD 5 ~ Patterns/Algebra

Through their explorations, play, and social interactions, children identify, repeat, and describe simple patterns using concrete objects.

Benchmarks

By the end of their preschool years, most children will

1. Sort, classify, and order objects by size and other properties

2. Identify simple patterns in the context of play or daily activities (such as "block, car, block, car") and use patterns to describe relationships between objects ("car follows block")

3. Predict, repeat, and extend a simple pattern in the context of play or daily activities ("dish, spoon, dish, spoon")

Promoting Understanding of Algebra

Stock the Math Area with manipulatives children can sort as they play, including counting bears, plastic toy animals, and cubes. Ask children to make patterns with the objects, beginning with very simple patterns, such as "cube, bear, cube, and bear." Start patterns yourself and ask children to finish them for you. Find patterns around the room with the children, such as patterns in wallpaper or on a piece of native cloth. Provide materials in other areas of the room children can use to make patterns, including the Art and Block Areas.

Make pattern mats by drawing a row of squares on plastic placemats and ask children to make patterns as they place one small object in each square. This activity can also be done by drawing squares on colored paper. Think out loud as you make patterns on the mats to model the process for the children. Encourage them to think out loud and talk about the pattern they are making as well.

Clap out patterns while singing songs, such as clapping twice, tapping twice, clapping twice, and tapping twice while singing "Twinkle, Twinkle, Little Star." Ask children to help you vary the patterns by choosing different motions they can perform with their hands and feet. Use actions to make patterns, such as "clap, touch your toes, clap, and touch your toes." Make "people patterns" with the children, asking one child to "stand"; the next to "sit, stand, sit"; or "boy, girl, boy, girl." Ask children to predict what will come next.

Supporting Children Who Are Bilingual Learners

Children who are learning a new language need many opportunities to experience mathematical words and concepts in order to be able to use them:

- Use a variety of hands-on manipulatives for children to touch and talk about as they work with them.
- Read counting books in both English and the home languages of the children. Include books that are written in both languages, such as *Uno, Dos, Tres: One, Two, Three* and *Diez Deditos/Ten Little Fingers, and Other Play Rhymes and Action Songs From Latin America.*
- Use meaningful opportunities throughout the day to count in English, Spanish, and other home languages of the children.
- Sing counting songs in English and other languages children are learning. Learn to count to 10 in the children's home languages and have everyone in the group join in counting and singing in these multiple languages.

- Use simple words to describe what you are doing as you make patterns, graphs, or do other mathematical work.
- Reinforce color words in English and other languages by describing simple patterns made with colored blocks or toys: *azul, rojo, azul, rojo,* and so on.

Working With Children's Individual Needs

Children who have special needs may require additional help in order to gain beginning mathematical skills. Current computer software, adaptive keyboards, and touch screens can help children see the concepts in different ways and allow them to practice their newly acquired skills. There are many things we can do to help all children be successful in mathematics:

- Make graphs out of actual objects so children can see the correspondence between the graph and what it represents. The objects can then be removed, and a picture of the object can be put in its place.
- Encourage children to use their fingers and other manipulatives when counting or doing any other mathematical activities.
- Teach children basic sign language to help them communicate their mathematical understanding. Use books such as *My Signing Book of Numbers* to introduce the signs for numbers.
- Give children large beads and manipulatives for making patterns.
- Make sure the Block Area is physically accessible to all children, including those in wheelchairs.
- Fabrics, sandpaper, and other textures can be glued to blocks and other shapes to help children differentiate the shapes and add to their sensory experience.
- Children can play with specialized cause-and-effect toys that will name a shape when that particular shape is pushed. Children with more involved disabilities can also use these toys, allowing them to be able to cause an effect with limited effort.

Summary

The preschool years are the optimal time for children to develop a foundation for mathematical thinking. The National Council of Teachers of Mathematics recommends several standard areas: Number and Operations, Geometry, Measurement, Data Analysis and Probability, and Algebra. Children need early hands-on experiences to develop understandings that lead to more advanced thinking over the years as they proceed through school. Enjoyable, developmentally appropriate experiences with mathematics can help children form positive attitudes toward mathematics and confidence in their ability to do it. Children will learn math concepts in many areas of the room as they build with blocks, measure, make patterns in the Art Area, work on the computer, and play in sand and water. Projects and themes, as well as daily activities, provide meaningful opportunities for children to learn and practice math skills. Adults need to be aware of mathematics standards and benchmarks that are appropriate for preschool-aged children and intentionally plan experiences that will help children grow in their understanding of these concepts.

8

Fostering Creativity Through the Arts

Children's creativity blossoms through rich experiences with the arts. Through the arts, children learn to express themselves and discover that they can represent their thoughts and ideas through many different media. The arts help children develop the concept that one thing can stand for another, that a symbol can represent an idea. This will help them in their understanding of literacy and mathematics, as they realize that a set of letters can stand for a name and a numeral represents a certain number of objects. The arts can be integrated into all areas of the curriculum; children can paint pictures to go along with stories they have dictated or create a dance to depict gently falling rain.

Children are able to communicate through art before they are able to express their ideas and emotions effectively with words. Art assists children in making meaning of their world and can increase their motivation to learn. Through art, children can develop self-esteem, learn new ways to solve problems, and learn about materials. Art experiences help children learn to accept and value their own work as well as that of others and to appreciate aesthetic elements in the world around them. Adults can nurture children's creativity by encouraging them to express their own thoughts, be original, and experiment. They can also create an inviting environment that nurtures children's explorations and ideas.

What Research and the Experts Tell Us
Young Children and the Arts

According to the American Council for the Arts in Education, the arts are basic to individual development and should be the heart of the educational curriculum for all young children. Children need time to play with and explore materials in order to understand how to use them. After extended periods of time working with the materials, they can begin to focus on what they would like to produce. There are several steps involved in the creative process:

(Continued)

(Continued)

1. Exploring
2. Focusing
3. Producing
4. Stopping, evaluating, or reworking

Young children spend most of their time at the exploring step. (Althouse, Johnson, & Mitchel, 2003; Lasky & Mukerji-Bergeson, 1980).

Provide abundant opportunities for children to explore with open-ended materials during the preschool years. Talk with children individually about what they would like to create, the materials they will use, and how they will carry out their plans. Encourage them to spend time developing their artwork and have a place where they can store their unfinished work to continue at a later time.

The Consortium of National Arts Education Associations developed standards for kindergarten through 12th grade in the areas of Music, Visual Arts, Theater, and Dance. Preschool standards for the Creative Arts outline skills and knowledge adults can help children acquire by the end of their preschool years. Below are sample preschool standards in the areas of Visual Arts, Music, Creative Movement, and Dramatic Play.

Sample Early Learning Guidelines for Creative Arts

STANDARD 1 ~ Visual Arts

Children use a variety of art materials for enjoyment and self-expression and demonstrate an appreciation for art.

STANDARD 2 ~ Music

Children engage in a variety of musical activities for enjoyment and self-expression and demonstrate an appreciation for music.

STANDARD 3 ~ Creative Movement

Children engage in a variety of creative movement activities for enjoyment and self-expression and demonstrate an appreciation for various forms of expressive movement.

STANDARD 4 ~ Dramatic Play

Children engage in pretend play for enjoyment and self-expression and demonstrate an appreciation for various forms of dramatic expression.

Fostering Creativity in the Arts Through Projects

The creative arts are an essential component of all projects. As children explore the project topic, they begin to understand that they can represent what they are learning through drawing, painting, working with clay, and many other art forms. As children create, we should celebrate their attempts and recognize that they are learning the process of representation.

A project may evolve, for example, as children begin asking questions about seeds after planting flower seeds with "adopted grandparent" volunteers from a nearby senior citizen center who came in to visit.

"Could these seeds grow in ketchup?"

"No, silly, it won't ever grow in ketchup!"

"Let's try syrup. It's brown and wet."

"I think it will grow in sand because sand is like dirt."

Extended inquiries might lead to a project on seeds, trees, or nature. Children can go outside and experience natural elements firsthand and draw, sketch, and paint pictures of what they are observing. Coming inside, then, children can further explore what they are learning with additional media. In the Dramatic Play Area, we can help children set up an area where they can further explore the topic. If children are exploring a nature-related topic, we might visit a nature center and invite a ranger or other expert in to speak about how they care for trees and other living things. Afterward, we could set up a nature center in the classroom, using a small, freestanding screen tent that allows for easy observation of the children inside. This area could also be set up with gauze or netting fabric draped over the top or around the area. Children could then suggest items, such as the following, to add to the nature center:

- Binoculars
- Field guides to plants, birds, and other animals
- Children's books on trees, birds, and other animals
- Flashlights
- Sleeping bag
- Aquarium with fish, frogs, or turtles

Reggio Emilia and the Arts

The schools in Reggio Emilia, Italy, are renowned for their approach to the arts with young children. They teach children art skills and techniques that will help them represent their ideas. They have a deep respect for children and their abilities. Children know they are trusted to make good choices and to use materials responsibly. In the Reggio Emilia approach, teachers speak of "the hundred languages of children," which include painting, sculpting, drawing, dancing, speaking, singing, and all the ways children learn to express themselves (Edwards, Forman, & Gandini, 1998). Children are engaged in using these many forms of language as they represent what they are learning throughout the long-term projects they are exploring. The children in the Reggio Emilia early childhood programs produce creative works of art, which have been shown in art museums around the world.

Designing the Environment

Set up an environment that invites children to create paintings, drawings, collages, and other works of art throughout the day. This can occur primarily in an Art Area stocked with appealing materials, which children can access independently.

Materials for the Art Area

- Easels
- Smocks or old shirts to cover clothing
- Variety of paints
- Variety of paper
- Washable water colors
- Washable markers
- Crayons
- Pencils
- Variety of brushes and other tools for painting
- Glue and paste
- Collage materials

The Art Area can be available to children most of the day, encouraging them to explore and create. Allowing children the opportunity to choose when and how much time to spend in the Art Area promotes creativity more than mandating a certain time or trying to do art activities with the entire group. As children visit the Art Area, you have more time to work with children individually or in small groups on their art; this is difficult if all children in the group are doing art at the same time. Children can also learn responsibility in the Art Area as they help with cleanup and putting materials away.

Set up a Music Area, where children have access to an assortment of instruments to play. Make sure there is plenty of space in the Music Area for children to move creatively.

Provide a Dramatic Play Area, where children can take on various roles. This area could be set up both indoors and outdoors and should include materials that will appeal to both boys and girls:

- Dress-up clothes
- Dolls and doll clothes
- Small furniture and props

Addressing Standards Through Engaging Experiences and Activities

The remainder of this chapter will provide sample standards and benchmarks for the creative arts as well as suggestions for addressing them through creative experiences and activities. These activities can be done in the context of a project or theme or can be used independently.

STANDARD 1 ~ Visual Arts

Children use a variety of art materials for enjoyment and self-expression and demonstrate an appreciation for art.

Benchmarks

By the end of their preschool years, most children will

1. Use a variety of materials for constructing, painting, drawing, and sculpting

2. Demonstrate enjoyment and confidence in their ability to freely plan and create artwork of their own design

3. Describe experiences, ideas, emotions, people, and objects represented in their artwork

4. Use words to describe their artwork in terms of color, line, shape, space, and texture

5. Demonstrate value and respect for their own artwork and that of their peers

6. Show appreciation for a variety of artwork, including that of their own cultures and communities as well as others

Promoting Visual Arts

Easels, paints, and other open-ended art materials should be available throughout the day. Special art materials can also be set out in the Art Area to help children learn new techniques and media. These can be available for extended periods of time to allow children to explore different variations in working with the materials. It is best to demonstrate the basics of *how* to use the materials but not limit *what* children will create with them. The process children go through to create their artwork is more important than their final products. While children are developing artistic skills, we want to make sure they can express themselves freely, without premade models to influence them. This will happen best

in a risk-free, accepting environment, where children can experiment and explore many different types of media.

Provide children many opportunities to draw throughout the day, with crayons, chalk, pencils, and markers. Make sure both thick and thin crayons and pencils are available. Occasionally, put these materials at the easel, providing a new way to explore the drawing process.

Children can paint with a variety of paints, brushes, and paper. At the beginning of the year, consider putting two or three primary colors of washable tempera paint at the easel. Encourage children to mix primary colors and predict what color will result from the mixing. Change the colors as the year goes by, adding and subtracting colors. Occasionally, add a container of white paint to the easel so children can mix it in with other colors to make pastels. This is fun to do in the spring. Children also enjoy mixing black with other colors and are often amazed to see the results when they mix black and white together. Teacher-supply stores and catalogs have a variety of paints in brilliant colors that children can use in their paintings. In addition to having paints available daily at the easel, from time to time, put containers of paint on the art table as well. Use a variety of colors, brushes, and paper.

Add texture and interest to tempera paint by adding ingredients such as the following:

- Coffee grounds
- Glitter
- Salt
- Sawdust
- Soap flakes
- Put out different materials for children to use as painting tools:
  - brushes of various lengths, widths, and sizes
  - foam brushes
  - toothbrushes
  - makeup brushes
  - cotton swabs

Printmaking offers a wealth of possibilities for children's exploration. Printmaking can be done using a variety of materials found around the home or classroom. Children can dip items in shallow containers of paint or washable inkpads and press them onto paper to make designs. Different items can be set out each week for children to explore:

Printmaking materials

- Strawberry baskets
- Cookie-cutters
- Potato masher
- Water bottles
- Thread spools
- Sponges cut in various shapes
- Suction cups
- Items from nature

Children enjoy working with clay and play dough. They also like taking part in making play dough. This can be done monthly in the Art Area with an interested group of children or more frequently as needed. Write out the recipe, using words and pictures on a large sheet of paper or poster board so children can follow the steps with you. Allow children to take part in measuring, pouring, stirring, and choosing the color. Multiple batches can be made in complementary colors, allowing children to learn more about color as they mix them. Use mess trays or other large plastic trays to contain the play dough while children play with it.

Paint with golf balls, tennis balls, or other small balls. Have children roll the balls in a shallow container of paint. Next, they can pick up the balls with a large spoon or set of tongs and drop the balls onto a piece of paper in a box. Children can tilt the box back and forth, watching the balls roll and the lines that develop.

Use other materials for painting, such as small toy cars. Children can dip the wheels of the car into a shallow container of paint and then move the car back and forth on a sheet of paper. Silk flowers can also be dipped in paint and used as a brush. Ask children to talk about the color, lines, shapes, and textures used in their painting.

Recipe for Play Dough

2 cups flour

1 cup salt

2 cups water

4 teaspoons cream of tartar

4 tablespoons oil

Food coloring

Mix ingredients together. Mixture will be a thin batter. Have an adult pour the batter into a skillet and cook on medium heat, stirring constantly until it thickens. Allow to cool.

Additional ingredients can be used to add color and scent, such as cinnamon, vanilla, powdered fruit drink mix, or dry, flavored gelatin.

Children enjoy kneading the play dough while it is still warm, but not hot to the touch.

Add a variety of tools and materials to increase interest with clay and play dough:

- Craft sticks
- Cookie-cutters
- Safety scissors
- Small mallets and rolling pins
- Materials from nature, such as pinecones, acorns, or seashells

Supply the Art Area with interesting materials for collages. Children can experiment combining different types of materials. Items for collages can include the following:

- Craft feathers
- Ribbon
- Fabric scraps
- Small pom-poms
- Shells
- Magazines with colorful pictures

Wood is another inviting material for children to explore. Many building supply stores are willing to donate scraps of wood that children can use. Initially, children can use sandpaper to sand the wood. After sanding, they can build creative structures, using glue to attach pieces of wood together. Children enjoy completing their constructions by painting them with tempera paint.

A Woodworking Area can be added to the room, where children can use hammers, screwdrivers, and saws to create additional constructions. Old desks, tables, or workbenches can be used as a woodworking surface. Soft woods are best for woodworking, and vices or C-clamps can be used to help children hold wood in place while they are working. Children should be given careful safety instructions on the use of each tool. They should be instructed to work in the area only when an adult is present and to wear safety goggles any time they are working. The Woodworking Area needs close supervision, so it is an area that should be available only when adults are free to spend time there.

Show respect and appreciation for children's art by displaying it at their level and making frames or mats to go around their artwork. Glue the artwork to a piece of colored construction paper, wallpaper, or tagboard that is larger than the child's picture. Frames can be made by folding a large piece of colored construction paper in half, cutting out the center of the paper slightly smaller than the child's artwork, and placing the child's artwork under the frame. Children can decorate the frames. Purchase old frames at rummage sales or secondhand stores, take out the glass, and insert children's artwork.

Ask children to tell you about their artwork, what they like about it and how they created it. Don't pass judgment on their art. Prompt them to think and talk about how they'd like to develop their ideas in future art endeavors.

Help children learn to appreciate art by sharing examples of pictures of works of art from many cultures, as well as your own community. These can be found in books, postcards, calendars, secondhand stores, and on the Internet. Include books with artwork in the Library Area and hang works of art on the walls. Some local libraries have paintings you can check out for extended periods of time. Encourage children to talk about what they

like about the art. Model your own sense of wonder about artwork by asking questions about how the artists created their work and what messages they were trying to convey. Prompt children to ask questions as well. Provide opportunities for children to use similar materials and techniques in the Art Area to create their own works of art. Then, talk with children about the ideas they are conveying and what they like about their artwork and that of other children.

STANDARD 2 ~ Music

Children engage in a variety of musical activities for enjoyment and self-expression and demonstrate an appreciation for music.

Benchmarks

By the end of their preschool years, most children will

1. Show enjoyment and participate in a variety of musical and rhythmic experiences, including singing, listening, and using musical instruments

2. Use music to communicate and express feelings, ideas, and experiences

3. Notice and imitate changes in vocal and instrumental music (high and low, loud and soft, etc.)

4. Show appreciation for a variety of music, including that of their own cultures and communities as well as others

Promoting Music

Enjoy singing with the children every day in large and small groups. Sing both indoors and outdoors. Teach simple songs with repetitive refrains. Write words to favorite songs on large chart paper and point to the words as you sing to encourage literacy development. Repeat familiar songs often, so children can sing them from memory. Have fun varying the tempo from fast to slow, the dynamics from loud to soft, and the pitch from high to low. Encourage children to notice the differences and follow your lead. Encourage children to compose creative words for familiar melodies that communicate their feelings and experiences. This word play, including the use of rhymes, can also help children develop their phonemic awareness. Singing provides other natural opportunities for children to grow in their phonemic awareness. Clapping their hands, tapping their toes, and keeping the beat with rhythm instruments while singing helps children distinguish the individual sounds in words. Hearing these individual sounds is a necessary component of phonemic awareness.

Create a Music Area, where children can play with a variety of instruments:

- Xylophones
- Multicultural instruments, including rain-sticks, maracas, and drums
- Rhythm instruments
- Triangles
- Bells

Include a CD or tape player with a variety of music for children to enjoy. Encourage children to play instruments in rhythm with the music.

Provide materials for children to make their own simple musical instruments. In the Art Area, supply crayons, markers, yarn, and paper plates with holes punched along the edges for children to make tambourines. Children can sew two plates together with yarn. Bind the end of the yarn with masking tape, to facilitate the sewing process. Just before the final stitches are completed, have children insert baby food jar lids or jingle bells between the two plates. To make an even better sound, use aluminum potpie pans taped together with duct tape. Children could decorate paper the size of the pan and tape it to the pan. Allow children to experiment with materials to put inside to make different sounds. Children could also add streamers or short ribbons to the outside of their tambourines and then play, keeping the beat to a variety of music. Talk with children about other items that could be used to make music. Keep in mind ideas such as playing pots and pans, wooden spoons, or making drums from oatmeal boxes and other household articles.

STANDARD 3 ~ Creative Movement

Children engage in a variety of creative movement activities for enjoyment and self-expression and demonstrate an appreciation for various forms of expressive movement.

Benchmarks

By the end of their preschool years, most children will

1. Participate in a variety of creative movement experiences, which could include dance and rhythmic activities

2. Explore ways to move imaginatively with and without music, such as stretching, galloping, twisting, bending, swaying, marching, and clapping

3. Use movement to communicate and express feelings, ideas, and experiences

4. Respond and move to the beat, tempo, and dynamics of music

5. Show appreciation for a variety of expressive movement, including that of their own cultures and communities as well as others

Promoting Movement

Play a variety of music children can dance or move to, such as marches, waltzes, polkas, reggae, Latin, folk, and jigs. To encourage movement or dance, try adding the following:

- Streamers
- Scarves
- Ribbons
- Tambourines
- Maracas
- Small bells that can be worn on the wrist, ankle, or waist
- Photos and paintings of dancers, such as paintings of ballet by Degas

Transform the Dramatic Play Area into a dance studio or set one up in another area of the room or outside. After visiting a dance studio and inviting dancers or family members in to do dances from several cultures, begin collecting items for the area, which might include the following:

- CD player with a variety of music for dance
- Dancing attire
- Skirts
- Mariachi pants and vests
- Dresses
- Tutus
- Capes
- Ballet slippers
- Tap shoes
- Cowboy boots

Children can help you make signs for the area, such as "Dance Studio."

Provide several opportunities in the daily schedule for movement activities. This could be at the end of story times, during transitions, or during closing rituals.

Invite parents and community members to share their traditional dances and teach the children simple movements. Ask them to play traditional instruments that children can move or dance to.

Encourage children to move in tempo with different types of music, allowing their bodies to respond to the rhythm, by swaying, bending, rocking, and using other imaginative movements. Sing favorite songs that have simple movements with the children, such as "Head, Shoulders, Knees, and Toes." Invite children to make up their own movements to songs and poems. Play classical music, such as "The Flight of the Bumblebee," and encourage children to express what they feel as they listen to the music.

STANDARD 4 ~ Dramatic Play

Children engage in pretend play for enjoyment and self-expression and demonstrate an appreciation for various forms of dramatic expression.

Benchmarks

By the end of their preschool years, most children will

1. Participate in a variety of spontaneous, imaginative play experiences alone or with others and create and engage in increasingly detailed and extended scenarios in their dramatic play

2. Use dramatic play to communicate and express feelings, ideas, and experiences

3. Use words and actions to imitate a variety of familiar stories, roles, and real-life or fantasy experiences

4. Use materials and props to represent objects in creative play

5. Show appreciation for a variety of dramatic experiences from their own cultures and communities as well as others, including storytelling, puppetry, and theater

Promoting Dramatic Play

Drama Boxes or Prop Boxes can be assembled to transform the Dramatic Play Area into an area where children can further explore various projects, themes, and children's books. Any boxes you have available, such as recycled paper boxes or clear plastic boxes, can be used, depending on the amount of items you have. Gather materials for a few boxes each year and label for future use.

Drama Boxes to Transform the Dramatic Play Environment

Restaurant (tablecloths, notepads, cash register, menus)

Flower shop (plastic flowers, small shovels, pots, cards, envelopes, markers)

Shoe shop (old shoes, slippers, skates, rulers, homemade measuring devices)

Bakery (play dough, rolling pins, pans, muffin pans, alphabet cookie cutters)

Pizza shop (materials donated by local pizza parlors, play dough, plastic cheese grater, cardboard rounds)

Archeology (great in combination with a sand table with sifters, brushes, magnifying glasses, maps)

Add multicultural clothes, dolls, posters, and fabrics as appropriate to the boxes.

Read favorite children's books and discuss the stories. Encourage children to act out the stories, retelling events in their own words. Children can gather props from around the room to enhance their dramatization. Invite local professionals to come in and demonstrate acting, miming, puppetry, and other areas of expertise they may have.

Supporting Children Who Are Bilingual Learners

The arts provide many opportunities for children to learn new words and express themselves in new languages:

- Children can easily learn songs in English and other languages, increasing their vocabularies. Songs can be repeated many times throughout the year, reinforcing these new words. Use pictures and props to help children understand the words they are singing.
- Make tapes of the children singing the same song in their home languages as well as English or other languages they might be learning. Children can listen to the tapes as they play.
- Equip the Housekeeping Area with household items and everyday objects; talk about the items with the children as they play. Change the Dramatic Play Area with each new project or theme to help children become familiar with new words as the props change.
- Encourage children to use the visual arts to express their thoughts and ideas along with the new words they are learning. Try to learn a few words in the children's languages so you can communicate basic concepts and messages.
- Store art materials on labeled shelves, where children can access them easily.

Working With Children's Individual Needs

The Arts provide experiences for children to develop their creativity and express themselves. These experiences are important for all children. Some children may need additional help to be able to participate fully. Many of these suggestions will be helpful for all children in our programs:

- Provide individual support to boost children's confidence and help them see value in their own work.
- Use large-handled paintbrushes.
- Provide painting mitts so children who do not like to have paint on their hands can experience finger painting.
- Provide specially adapted scissors.
- Make homemade tabletop easels for children who have difficulty standing or working at the easel.
- For those who have difficulty singing, provide instruments for them to play and encourage them to hum along, if possible, to boost their participation in group musical activities.
- For those who have difficulty with movement, encourage them to move any parts of their bodies they can.

- For those who have hearing impairments, make sure they can feel the beat of music. Turn up the bass on CD players. Invite children to feel instruments as they are played.
- Make sure the Dramatic Play, Music, and Art Areas are physically accessible to all children.

Summary

The arts can be integrated into all areas of the curriculum. Standards in the areas of Visual Arts, Music, Creative Movement, and Dramatic Play outline what children should know and be able to do in the arts. Preschool programs can help children develop in these areas through interesting projects and activities. Providing an environment where children can freely explore a variety of art materials inspires children to develop their creativity. Emphasis should be placed on the process children go through to create their art, rather than on the final products. An area with musical instruments, music on CD or tape, scarves, and room to move will help children learn about and enjoy music and communicate through their music and movement. Changing the props in the Dramatic Play Area to complement projects and themes provides children with opportunities to discover and grow in multiple ways. Children learn to express themselves and represent their ideas through the arts as they explore topics in depth.

9

Promoting Physical Development and Healthy Lifestyles

Children's physical development and health in the early years have a profound effect on their future. Helping children gain knowledge and positive attitudes about exercise and eating will help them make good choices and form healthy habits that can last a lifetime. Children also need to know safe practices and how to implement them in their daily lives.

Healthy children are better able to take advantage of learning opportunities. Good health and physical well-being also bring happiness to children's lives. The Council on Physical Education for Children of the National Association for Sport and Physical Education (NASPE) stated that "the appropriate approach for [children 3–5 years of age] is to focus on fundamental motor skills, movement concepts, and the *joy of moving* to assist the child's motor, cognitive, emotional, and social development" (Council on Physical Education for Children for NASPE, 2000, p. 5, emphasis added). NASPE has developed the following guidelines for physical activity:

1. Preschoolers should accumulate at least one hour of daily planned physical activity.

2. Preschoolers should engage in at least 60 minutes and up to several hours of daily, spontaneous physical activity and should not be sedentary for more than one hour at a time.

3. Preschoolers should develop competence in movement skills that are the building blocks for more complex movement tasks.

4. Preschoolers should have indoor and outdoor areas that meet or exceed recommended safety standards for performing large-muscle activities.

5. Individuals responsible for the well-being of preschoolers should be aware of the importance of physical activity and facilitate the child's movement skills.

Planned physical activity should be thoughtfully developed and guided by adults, allowing for children to choose a variety of activities that will allow them to play and enjoy movement and exercise. These activities can be done during outdoor play, as well as during large- and small-group time. This chapter presents many ideas that can be used in planning.

SOURCE: Reprinted from *Active Start: A Statement of Physical Activity Guidelines for Children Birth to Five Years* (2002), with permission from the National Association for Sport and Physical Education (NASPE), 1900 Association Drive, Reston, VA 20191, USA.

What Research and the Experts Tell Us

Physical Development

Modeling is a powerful way to help children learn. Children need to see adults exercising, moving, walking, eating healthy foods, and enjoying these activities (NASPE, 2002). Parent involvement is also very important in helping children develop large and small motor skills. Research has also found that practice is essential for children to develop both fine and gross motor skills. Experts suggest varying activities to keep them fun and enjoyable and to include play as well as planned activities. Research has shown that growth in physical development and health positively affects all other areas of development. Children need to be active participants in order to develop skills (NASPE, 2002).

Preschool standards for Physical Development and Health outline the skills, knowledge, and understandings that most children can acquire by the end of their preschool years.

Sample Early Learning Guidelines for Physical Development and Health

Standard 1 ~ Gross Motor

Children engage in play and movement to develop gross (large) motor skills.

Standard 2 ~ Fine Motor

Children engage in play and interesting experiences to develop fine motor skills.

Standard 3 ~ Health and Safety

Children engage in play and interesting experiences to develop healthy habits and safe practices.

Promoting Physical Development and Healthy Lifestyles Through Projects

Children can learn a great deal about healthy lifestyles and grow in their physical development while working on projects. In a project related to nature, children can learn how plants grow and where we get our fruits, vegetables, and other healthy foods. Projects also give children opportunities to refine their fine motor skills as they use drawings, paintings, and clay or play dough constructions to represent what they are learning.

If children have been spending large blocks of time playing with toy animals and talking about various animals, you might choose to do a project related to this topic. You may hear frequent conversations such as the following:

"I like horses. I like to ride it. I like to feed horses."

"I think about butterflies, bumblebees, and yellow jackets. The bumblebees and yellow jackets are stinging animals. Spiders are biting animals."

"I think buffalos maybe are grass collectors maybe? Like grass-collecting machines?"

"I like kitties. They look like flowers. They play with people. But they bite when people try to pick them up!"

In a project on animals, children can develop their large motor skills as they learn about the movements of various animals and then imitate these actions. After reading a book such as *From Head to Toe,* which describes animal movements, children can investigate motions such as the following:

- Standing on one foot like a flamingo
- Hopping like a bunny or kangaroo
- Leaping like a frog
- Climbing like a monkey
- Galloping like a horse
- Kicking like a donkey
- Swaying like an elephant
- Sliding like a snake
- Crawling like a turtle
- Curling into a ball like a hedgehog

Photographs of the children's explorations could be made into a book, with one child's photograph on each page accompanied by a sentence such as "A flamingo stands on one foot, can you do it?" or "Dominique can crawl like a turtle." Children could also make their own illustrations for the book.

Designing the Environment

Design the environment to promote physical development. Arrange the room so children feel invited to move and exercise and there is room for them to do this. Display materials in

an appealing manner that calls out to children to play. Physically active children have a better chance of being healthy later in life. Our role is to prepare an engaging environment with motivating activities, in which children actively participate and are challenged to advance toward their potential (Sanders, 2002).

To promote physical activity, the inside environment could include the following:

- Large areas for movement
- Child-sized furniture and equipment
- Plastic padded mats for exercising
- Different sizes and types of balls
  - foam balls
  - stringy (koosh) balls
  - beach balls
  - large exercise balls
- Low balance beams or long wooden blocks that can be used as a balance beam
- Beanbags
- Parachute
- Objects for making an obstacle course

To promote physical activity, the outside environment could include the following:

- Large areas where children can play outside safely
- Child-safe jungle gym
- Low balance beams

- Tricycles, other wheeled vehicles, and bike helmets
- Plastic racquets and balls that are soft
- Baby buggies, strollers, and wagons to push and pull
- Surfaces of varying heights

Have an area in the room where children can be involved in movement activities. Set up different stations, which could be changed weekly, depending on children's interests. These stations could be done inside or outside and could include the following:

- Tossing a beanbag
- Dropping a scarf or piece of fabric and kicking it as it comes to the ground
- Making a grid with tape on the floor where children can hop on one foot between the tape marks
- Marking out a path for children to follow, so they can throw a beanbag along the path, run to pick it up where it lands, throw it again, and repeat.
- Walking on tiptoes around the outside of a hula hoop
- Walking on a balance beam
- Standing on one foot for 5 seconds
- Stretching and simple exercises on mats with pictures or photographs depicting each exercise

A variety of interest areas can be designed to promote physical development:

- Dramatic Play Area
  - Brooms
  - Dolls and doll clothes for dressing
  - Dress-up clothes
  - Dolls with zippers, buttons, and snaps
- Dollhouse with small multicultural dolls, furniture, and animal figures
- Sensory table with sand or water and toys
- Art Area
  - crayons
  - washable markers
  - paintbrushes
  - colored pencils
  - safety scissors
- Music Area with musical instruments
  - xylophone to strike with mallets
  - tone blocks
  - rhythm sticks
  - tambourine
  - triangle
  - multicultural instruments
- Writing Area
  - pencils
  - washable markers
  - rubber stamps with washable inkpads
- Table toys
  - Puzzles
  - Peg-Boards and pegs
  - Large beads for stringing
  - Small blocks, such as Duplos®, ABC blocks, and bristle blocks
  - Manipulatives that snap together, such as Unifix Cubes
  - Sewing table with lacing cards

Addressing Standards Through Engaging Experiences and Activities

For children to develop lifelong healthy lifestyles, they need to form positive attitudes and habits in the early years. Interesting, fun and developmentally appropriate activities and projects can promote this development. The following section provides sample benchmarks for each of the Physical Development and Health Standards, along with engaging activities that can be used in the context of a project or theme or used independently. Adults can use these activities in their plans to help each child make progress in these areas.

Standard 1 ~ Gross Motor

Children engage in play and movement to develop gross (large) motor skills.

Benchmarks

By the end of their preschool years, most children will

1. Participate in play and movement activities and describe how physical activity contributes to their overall health ("Exercise helps make me strong!")

2. Demonstrate locomotor skills by walking, running, hopping, galloping, marching, and climbing

3. Demonstrate stability, flexibility, and balance by standing on one foot, turning, stretching, bending, rolling, balancing, stopping, jumping, and twisting

4. Demonstrate increasing coordination when pedaling, throwing, catching, kicking, bouncing objects, and hitting objects with racquets or paddles

5. Demonstrate increasing body strength and endurance in play and movement experiences

Promoting Gross Motor Development

Play noncompetitive games and physical activities with children to promote development of motor skills. Keep all children actively involved throughout the activities to extend the amount of time they are engaged and moving. Ask them to plant their feet on the ground and try not to move them. Then, try stretching, bending forward and backward and side to side, turning, twisting, touching the ground, and reaching for the sky. Children could pretend to be palm trees, standing still and then swaying in the wind.

Provide opportunities for children to play with balls and rolling other cylindrically shaped objects, such as oatmeal boxes, empty paper towel rolls, or empty plastic bottles of various sizes. Children can also try kicking these objects around the room and talking about the differences they observed. Tape the outline of various shapes on the floor and ask children to jump from one shape to another.

Take walks with the children, varying the pace and distance. This can be done inside in hallways or a room if it isn't possible to go outside. Give children opportunities to walk along paths that are straight, zigzagged, and curved. Provide opportunities for children to push and pull wagons, wheelbarrows, strollers, and carts.

Set up an obstacle course so that children can go over, under, around, and through an array of objects. Include large cardboard boxes with both ends opened or see-through tunnels that children can crawl through. Help children practice their stability by asking them to walk on balance beams, long wooden blocks set out on the floor, sidewalk cracks, or chalk lines on the ground. They can do this moving both forward and backward. Provide opportunities for children to practice using stairs.

Music can add motivation and excitement to movement activities. Play "Follow the Leader," having the adult start using different actions, such as bending and jumping. Then, have children take turns being the leader, using a variety of actions. While children are playing, they can be singing, "We're following the leader, the leader, the leader, we're following the leader wherever she may go." March to various kinds of music, occasionally adding rhythm instruments, streamers, or scarves. Enjoy a variety of dances, such as the twist and Hokey Pokey. Ask family members to teach simple dance movements from their cultures. Play games where children can practice moving to music quickly, slowly, and stopping when the music stops. Move furniture or go outside if more room is needed.

Standard 2 ~ Fine Motor

Children engage in play and interesting experiences to develop fine motor skills.

Benchmarks

By the end of their preschool years, most children will

1. Participate in play and movement activities that enhance fine motor development
2. Demonstrate eye-hand coordination through activities such as stringing large beads and completing simple puzzles
3. Practice self-help skills, such as buttoning, zipping, and snapping
4. Display strength and control while using a variety of manipulative materials, including scissors, pencils, crayons, small toys, and connecting blocks

Promoting Fine Motor Development

Set up interest areas where children have many opportunities to practice their fine motor skills. This can include a puzzle table, math manipulatives, magnifying glasses, small blocks, and construction toys. Occasionally, provide a Woodworking Area, where children can use tools such as hammers and screwdrivers with adult supervision. Include dress-up clothes in the Dramatic Play Area, where children can practice buttoning, snapping, and zipping. Encourage children to dress themselves when going outside. In the Art and Writing Areas, give children opportunities to use crayons, washable markers, chalk, paintbrushes of various sizes, pencils, and other tools.

Offer experiences for children to use play dough and clay. Provide a variety of objects for them to use while playing with the play dough, such as cookie-cutters, craft sticks, old safety scissors, and rolling pins. This play will increase strength as well as fine motor skills.

Enjoy fingerplays and songs with the children, such as "The Itsy Bitsy Spider," "Five Little Monkeys," and "Where Is Thumbkin?" Teach children simple sign language to use with favorite songs. Add hand and finger motions to other songs to add enjoyment.

Standard 3 ~ Health and Safety

Children engage in play and interesting experiences to develop healthy habits and safe practices.

TRY THIS!

Give children spray bottles with colored water they can spray on paper outside or squirt color on snow or sand. They can also use the bottles to spray water on grass, trees, and other plants, strengthening their fine motor skills as they repeat the squeezing motion. Bring art and writing materials outside, if possible, for a different experience. Attach paper to clipboards, cardboard boxes, fences, or walls.

Benchmarks

By the end of their preschool years, most children will

1. Recognize and identify nutritious foods

2. Independently practice personal care and self-help skills, including washing hands, brushing teeth, toileting, dressing, and eating

One way some of the young children of Ecuador practice their fine motor skills is by working with flour, water, and a rolling pin. The children mix the flour and water together on the table and spend time rolling out the mixture with a small rolling pin. Even classrooms with only a small amount of materials may have enough rolling pins for a number of children to do this at one time.

3. Know how and when to alert adults to dangerous situations

4. Recognize basic safety symbols, including stop signs, red lights, and poison symbols

5. Follow street, vehicle, and bike safety rules, such as looking both ways before crossing and using car safety seats and bike helmets

6. Know how to respond safely in emergency situations, such as a fire or tornado, and in the presence of strangers or dangerous objects

Promoting Health and Safety

Children can learn about healthy foods by helping to prepare healthy snacks, such as fruit salad, freshly squeezed juice, or carrots. Visit Spatulatta, Cooking 4 Kids on Line (http://www.spatulatta.com) for easy recipes children can help prepare.

Serve a wide variety of healthy foods from many cultures, particularly those represented in your community. Introduce new foods on several different occasions to encourage children to experience new tastes, flavors, and textures. Have discussions with the children to help them distinguish foods that are healthy from those that are not. Provide examples of nutritious foods in the Dramatic Play Area, using plastic fruits and vegetables or clean, empty grocery items, such as milk jugs.

Provide opportunities for children to practice self-help skills. During mealtime, allow children to practice pouring, using utensils, and serving themselves food. Use pitchers, bowls, and platters that are easy for children to handle on their own. Promote self-help skills by encouraging children to wash and dry their own hands and brush their teeth after meals. Supply a step stool if needed. Provide a sanitary place where each child can store his or her own toothbrush.

Teach children basic safety concepts. Accidents are reported to be one of the most frequent causes of death among young children. Encourage children to wear bike helmets and use car safety seats. Provide information to parents on the importance of helmets, car seats, and other safety concerns. Include safety signs and symbols in the Dramatic Play Area and Block Area and talk with children about what they mean. Point out safety signs outside as well. When walking, practice looking both ways and using the crosswalk when crossing the street. Teach children not to touch dangerous objects, such as matches, fireworks, guns, knives, and other sharp objects. They also need to know the importance of taking medicine given to them only by a trusted adult. Talk with children about the dangers of playing in cars, old appliances, or trunks or going into pipes or

Recipe for Homemade Banana Pudding

Have each child do the following:

Mash ½ small, ripe banana in a small bowl.

Add 3 tablespoons all-natural applesauce.

Stir in 1 tablespoon plain or vanilla yogurt.

Enjoy!

openings they see in the ground. Let children know that if they see or experience any kind of danger, emergency, or health problem, they should tell an adult immediately. Teach children never to talk to strangers and provide suggestions they can follow if a stranger tries to abduct them, such as calling out loudly, "This is not my daddy or mommy" and running to a trusted adult.

Review basic safety procedures in case of emergency. Have an evacuation plan and practice "safety drills" with the children, talking about and focusing on "what we need to do to be safe," rather than putting the focus on the danger. Let children know they don't need to worry or be fearful, because they know they can do what they have rehearsed and follow their trusted adult to get out of harm's way. Children who live in areas prone to disasters may need additional training on what to do in case of natural disasters, such as floods, hurricanes, earthquakes, tornadoes, or even volcanic eruption. The American Red Cross has information online (http://www.redcross.org) that can be shared with children, including materials that can help families prepare for disasters.

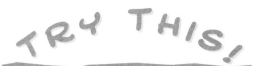

Try growing healthy fruits and vegetables inside, such as cherry tomatoes or potatoes that children can later eat. To grow potatoes, begin with an old potato with eyes that have sprouted. Cut the potato into large pieces, making sure that each piece has a sprout. Plant the pieces in a container with soil and place near a window where it will receive plenty of sunlight.

Supporting Children Who Are Bilingual Learners

Activities related to health and physical development provide a meaningful context for children learning new languages. Use descriptive words to identify foods and activities. Prepare healthy foods from a variety of cultures, including the home cultures of the children.

- Involve children in preparing healthy snacks and meals from the home cultures of the children. In making a recipe, such as tacos, children can be involved in preparing ingredients and assembling their own servings.
- Become familiar with key words and phrases in the children's languages so you can communicate basic messages with them, including words related to their health and safety.
- Sing "The Hokey Pokey" and "Head, Shoulders, Knees, and Toes" and play "Simon Says" with the children, using both English and other languages to identify body parts and commands.
- Play games using beanbags of various colors. Ask children to toss, catch, or hop over designated colors, while saying the name of the color in several languages.
- Consider asking families to share traditional foods and describe them to the children. Children can then take turns passing out these healthy foods and repeating a simple phrase, such as "My friend, enjoy a ____." Children can respond with "Thank-you." These exchanges could take place in several languages.

Recipe for Classic Filipino Pancit

(from http://www.fooddownunder.com)

Ingredients

1 cup chicken broth or vegetable broth

1/4 cup vegetable oil

2 tablespoons soy sauce

1 small sweet onion

1 small cabbage, shredded

1 clove of garlic, minced

2 medium carrots, chopped

2 medium celery stalks, chopped

4 ounces rice sticks (py mai fun comes in an 8 oz. package)

Additional: soy sauce and sweet & sour sauce for seasoning

Instructions

In a separate pan of hot water, soak the rice sticks until soft, then cut with scissors into lengths 2 to 3 inches long. In a skillet, using medium heat, sauté onions in the vegetable oil. Add garlic, cabbage, carrots, and celery, and stir together. Add broth and soy sauce while cooking and stirring. Cook until the vegetables are tender; the liquids should be almost all absorbed. Add drained rice sticks to the vegetables, mix together, and cook until heated through (about 1–2 minutes). Serve and season to taste with additional soy sauce and sweet & sour sauce.

Pancit (or poncit) can be served as a vegetable dish or can also be mixed with cooked shrimp, strips of beef, chicken breast, pork, or tofu.

Working With Children's Individual Needs

It is important to design our curriculum so that all children can participate as fully as possible in activities and feel successful. For this to happen, we need to adapt the environment and activities to meet individual capabilities. Some children will need a great deal of assistance, while others will need only a small amount of additional support. Creating an atmosphere where all children feel they are an important part of the group, and respect and help each other, will help all children feel successful. Many of the following suggestions will be helpful for all children in our programs:

- Adapt activities so all children can participate. This might include running a shorter route or throwing a different object, so that each child feels capable.
- Provide many opportunities for children to practice skills and build strength. Vary the setting, equipment, and materials.
- Use pictures and modeling to demonstrate concepts.
- Adapt writing instruments with rubber grips or spongy padding around them. Furnish thick brushes, crayons, and pencils. Fasten handles to objects to make it easier for children to hold onto them. Offer knobbed puzzles, switches, and adaptive scissors.
- Position rubber mats or other nonslip surfaces under paper, puzzles, and other objects to keep them from slipping. Use them under plates and use eating utensils that are easy to grasp.
- Provide balls that are easy to use, including large balls and plastic balls with holes that may be easier to grip.
- Attach a glove to a small paddle or racquet so children can grasp it more easily.
- Make certain equipment is the correct size and placed so children can take part safely. Materials such as standers and adapted seating and supports can be used if needed.

Summary

Helping children develop healthy attitudes toward exercise and eating can build a foundation for future healthy lifestyles. An engaging environment that invites play and active participation can provide children with opportunities to develop in the preschool standard areas of Gross Motor, Fine Motor, and Health and Safety. Involving children in preparing nutritious snacks and meals can help children form better attitudes toward healthy eating. Participating in daily exercise, walking, and enjoyable movement activities can help children learn to appreciate the value of these pursuits. Children can also develop motor skills and understanding of healthy habits and safe practices by participating in focused studies or long-term projects, in which they can learn these things in a meaningful way.

10

Putting It All Together

The early years of life are the optimal time to help children build a firm foundation for life and learning. During these years, children form attitudes toward learning as well as about themselves as learners. When children enjoy learning and see themselves as capable and successful, they seek out opportunities to spend more time in engaging learning experiences, which leads to greater achievement. We want children to develop a real joy in learning and sense of wonder that will sustain their desire to learn throughout their lives. This requires the support of caring adults who intentionally plan experiences that will nurture these attitudes: "If a child is to keep alive his inborn sense of wonder he needs the companionship of at least one adult who can share it, rediscovering with him the joy, excitement and mystery of the world we live in" (Carson, 1965, p. 54). Quality preschool standards assist adults in planning curricula that will help children progress in their development.

Addressing Standards in Developmentally Appropriate Ways

Developmentally appropriate preschool standards outline the knowledge, skills, and understandings most children can learn in a supportive environment. With guidance, 3-year-olds will begin to make progress toward the standards, and most children will meet them by the end of their preschool years. In their joint position statement on *Early Learning Standards,* the National Association for the Education of Young Children and the National Association of Early Childhood Specialists in State Departments of Education (2002) stated that "early learning standards can be a valuable part of a comprehensive, high-quality system of services for young children, contributing to young children's educational experiences and to their future success" (p. 2).

Supportive adults can promote children's development toward meeting standards by implementing these key elements:

1. Design an engaging environment with interest areas and motivating materials that promote active participation.

2. Create a community of learners in which children feel welcomed and part of a community that cares about them.

3. Provide a curriculum that actively engages children in learning and exploration, with intentional teaching on the part of adults, including projects, focused studies, or themes.

4. Use authentic assessment while children are engaged in play and everyday activities to provide information about their current levels of understanding and what they need in order to move forward.

5. Build reciprocal relationships with families, in which there is a sharing of information and mutual respect.

Standards provide us with a *path*, a direction that guides our teaching and what children are learning. They should not be viewed as a pass/fail measurement. It is important that we keep in mind that our goal is to help children develop and grow in their understandings, not merely be able to repeat information back to us.

There are many developmentally appropriate experiences we can offer children that will help them make progress in meeting preschool standards. This chapter provides sample projects and themes that will engage children and help them build a foundation for successful learning. It also offers suggestions on how to support children's transition to kindergarten as they finish their preschool years.

Addressing Standards and Benchmarks Through Projects, Studies, and Themes

Exploring a topic of interest through a project, focused study, or theme helps children understand concepts in a meaningful way. As children listen to books, create art, visit field sites, and spend time in interest areas related to the study, they see the topic through the lens of literacy, art, math, science, and other fields. They gain a better understanding of the topic through all of these perspectives.

Choosing a Topic

Reviewing early learning guidelines when considering a topic to investigate will allow you to make sure the topic will address many of the guidelines. Check off standards and benchmarks as you address them, keeping in mind that children need many opportunities to learn a new concept. Assess children on an ongoing basis to determine which standards and benchmarks they need additional experiences with before deciding on a topic of study.

Science and social studies provide good topics for a project, focused study, or theme. Almost any area connected to nature can make a good topic, depending on the interests of the children and the resources you have available. Possible areas might include trees, flowers, water, or animal homes.

As children explore the topic, they will have the opportunity to gain skills in every subject area. Of course, there will be a host of science standards and benchmarks that can be met while working on a nature-related topic, such as animal homes. As children listen to books and visitors, walk outside looking for nests and webs, and construct their own animal homes, they will have the opportunity to meet benchmarks in every one of the science standard areas, as well as all other content areas. A quality topic in the area of social studies will meet standards and benchmarks in every area as well.

Planning

When planning, think about books you might read related to the topic, field visits you might take, visitors you could invite, opportunities for dramatic play, and other experiences children might have throughout the study. Family members are often delighted to be asked to come in and share a particular area of expertise they may have. It is important that any visitor or expert you invite to speak with the children be able to do it on the children's level. Talk with visitors before they come to help them understand what would be appropriate and interest the children. Encourage them to bring pictures or items children can see and touch to enhance their experience. Children enjoy visiting field sites related to the topic and learn a great deal from these opportunities. Sites need to be checked out ahead of time to make sure they are safe and appropriate. Investigating different locations in your own building, yard, block, or neighborhood are often the best choices. When possible, taking the children in small groups allows them to get more out of the visit. They are able to ask more questions and get more personalized attention. Individuals at the field sites often prefer this as well.

Sample Projects, Focused Studies, or Themes

Children's interests should guide our choice of a topic to investigate. Possible topics might include animals and their homes, water, food, and clothes.

Animals and Their Homes

- *Possible field visits:* walks outside to find nests, insect homes, and webs; nature center; farm; zoo with natural habitats
- *Visitors or experts:* ranger, zookeeper, farmer, rancher, parent
- *Opportunities for dramatic play:* nature center, animal homes

Turn the Dramatic Play Area into a nature center by setting up a screen tent, either inside or outdoors. Children could make a variety of animal homes to display in the nature center, including bird nests, birdhouses, spider webs, and dens.

Provide children with a wide range of materials to use in building the homes: wooden blocks, bits of fabric, string, yarn, play dough, paper, and cardboard boxes. Children can also make animal houses outside with various natural materials, such as leaves, mud, clay, sand, and twigs.

Provide opportunities for children to try weaving with natural materials to form a nest, as some birds do. Children could help set up an aquarium or fishbowl after discussing what would make a good home for a fish. They could also observe the activity in an ant farm.

- Books: *Animal Homes; Some Sleep Standing Up; What Do You Call a Termite Home? And Other Animal Homes; Is Your Mama a Llama?; Owl Babies; The Very Busy Spider; In a Tree; At the Pond; In the Tall, Tall Grass*

A project or focused study on animal homes might lead to a study of water if children display interest in this topic.

Water

- *Possible field visits:* puddle, pond, science/discovery museum, aquarium
- *Visitors or experts:* ranger, naturalist, parent, health care professional
- *Opportunities for dramatic play:* kitchen area, pond

Encourage children to explore how living things need and use water. The Dramatic Play Area could become a kitchen, where children can experience water's properties while washing plastic dishes and bathing dolls in a water table or plastic container.

The Dramatic Play Area could also be transformed into a pond, using blue fabric or paper on the floor or around the area. Children could suggest items to add to the pond, such as toy ducks, fish, frogs, and plants.

At the water table or in a container of water, children can explore the physical properties of water with tubes, funnels, and water wheels. They can make predictions and experiment with a variety of objects that sink and float.

Children can explore plants' need for water by growing flowers and vegetables and watering them with eyedroppers. As the project evolves, discussions about the importance of water to our health can be incorporated.

- Books: *A Cool Drink of Water; In the Small, Small Pond; Swimmy; Water Dance; In the Rain With Baby Duck; Amy Loves the Rain; Water*

A project or focused study on water might lead to a study of food.

Food

- *Possible field visits:* kitchen, garden, grocery store, farm, farmers' market, bakery
- *Visitors or experts:* gardener, parent, grocer, farmer, nutritionist
- *Opportunities for dramatic play:* health food store, grocery store, kitchen, bakery, restaurant

Children can explore a variety of food topics, including growing and preparing foods, healthy eating, and foods from many cultures. Parents can be involved in this topic by preparing traditional foods with the children. They can also share expertise they may have in gardening or other interests, skills, or occupations related to food or healthy eating.

- Books: *Bread, Bread, Bread; Eating the Alphabet; The Carrot Seed; How Are You Peeling? Food With Moods; Lunch; Handa's Surprise; Vegetables in the Garden; Crunch Munch; Eat Up, Gemma; The Hungry Little Boy; Lunch; Today Is Monday; Yoko*

As children explore food from other cultures, they may become interested in finding out more about clothing worn by people around the world.

Clothes

- *Possible field visits:* coat closet, neighborhood clothing store, dressmaker, fabric stores
- *Visitors or experts:* family members from a variety of cultures showing traditional dress, dressmaker, tailor
- *Opportunities for dramatic play:* clothing store, shoe store, fabric store, theater, clothing worn by community helpers

Children enjoy dressing up in the Dramatic Play Area and wearing aprons, dresses, suits, shoes, and other attire. They can explore roles of community helpers as they dress in uniforms worn by these individuals. They can also learn more about their own growth and development as they play with clothing worn by babies, children, and adults.

Adding clothing from a variety of cultures allows children to learn about them as well. Children can help convert this area into a clothing store, fabric store, or theater, where they can explore making clothes or costumes with fabrics, yarn, ribbon, scarves, and other accessories. This will also give them opportunities to practice their fine motor skills as they button, zip, and work with the fabrics and clothes. Families can contribute articles of clothing, accessories, and fabric remnants.

Children's study of clothing can also lead to an awareness of the differences in the seasons, as they discover different types of clothing suited for various types of weather.

- Books: *Jamela's Dress; Max's Dragon Shirt; Shoes From Grandpa; Jingle Dancer; Joseph Had a Little Overcoat; Animals Should Definitely Not Wear Clothing; How Do I Put It On?; This Is the Baby; You'll Soon Grow Into Them, Titch*

Supporting the Transition to Kindergarten

Children will be more successful in school if they have a smooth transition from their preschool years to kindergarten. Planning the transition from preschool to kindergarten will help prepare children and families.

What Research and the Experts Tell Us

Transition to Kindergarten

In *Successful Kindergarten Transition: Your Guide to Connecting Children, Families, and School,* authors Robert Pianta and Marcia Kraft-Sayre (2003) have provided a wealth of information that can help ease children's transitions to kindergarten. Relationships are the key to successful transitions, including relationships between the child and the teacher, the child and the parent, the child and other children, teacher and parents, and relationships with the community. Working with parents is essential; their perceptions of school influence their children's attitudes. Collaboration between teachers, principals, families, preschool teachers, child care providers, and other professionals is fundamental. Planning for transitions should be made collaboratively and could begin a year before the actual transition, with a timeline outlining events that will take place (Pianta & Kraft-Sayre, 2003).

Collaborating With Kindergarten Teachers

There are several activities that help children transition into kindergarten with more confidence and positive anticipation. Those working with preschool children can collaborate with kindergarten teachers and administrators to plan events throughout the year prior to entry. When possible, taking children to visit their future kindergarten classrooms before the start of the school year can make a tremendous difference in their comfort levels. During the visit, children can meet with the kindergarten teachers and see the kinds of activities children do in the classroom. These visits could be done in small groups with their preschool or child care providers or could be done individually with parents.

Collaborating With Families

Calendars can be given to families, with simple activities they can do with their children throughout the summer before kindergarten. Each day of the summer months could contain a suggestion, such as *Plant seeds today; Make a visit to your local library; Ask your child to help you set the table; Make a snack together;* and *Look for shapes in the clouds.* Every day could include the reminder: *Read a book together today.*

There are a number of books you can read to children to help them understand what kindergarten might be like. This will help reduce anxiety and make for an easier transition. These books include the following:

- *The Night Before Kindergarten,* by Natasha Wing
- *Miss Bindergarten Gets Ready for Kindergarten,* by Joseph Slate
- *Welcome to Kindergarten,* by Anne Rockwell
- *Kindergarten Kids,* by Ellen B. Senisi
- *Tom Goes to Kindergarten,* by Margaret Wild
- *The Kissing Hand,* by Audrey Penn

Final Thoughts

Preschool standards can help guide our work with young children. They describe the skills, knowledge, and understandings that will form a firm foundation for later learning. Children will reach standards best through experiences that invite them to play, while nurturing their sense of wonder and joy in learning.

All children are born ready to learn; our goal is that all children will be ready to be successful. According to Pianta and Walsh (1996),

Children are ready for school when, for a period of several years, they have been exposed to consistent stable adults who are emotionally invested in them, to a physical environment that is safe and predictable; to regular routines and rhythms of activity; to competent peers; and to materials that stimulate their exploration and enjoyment of the world from which they derive a sense of mastery. (p. 34)

All children need and deserve relationships, environments, and experiences that will help them learn, as well as develop a true sense of wonder and joy in learning.

Resources

Signs for Interest Areas

These signs can be personalized with your own state standards, enlarged, mounted on cardboard, laminated, and hung in the appropriate areas of the room. You could also add a photograph of your children playing in each area or simply photocopy and use.

READING AREA

Here we are learning skills and strategies

to get meaning from print.

We are learning to enjoy books and reading.

WRITING AREA

Here we are learning to use writing and drawing

as a means of communication

and representing our ideas.

LISTENING AREA

Here we are learning to listen

to environmental sounds and conversations

and learning phonological awareness.

MATH AREA

Here we are learning about

Number Sense and Operations

Shapes/Geometry

Measurement

Making Sense of Data

Patterns/Algebra

SCIENCE/DISCOVERY AREA

Here we are learning about

Science as Inquiry

Physical Science

Life Science

Earth and Space Science

Science and Technology

Science, Environment, and Society

as we explore and investigate through play.

ART AREA

Here we are learning to use a variety of art materials

and demonstrate an appreciation for art.

DRAMATIC PLAY AREA

Here we engage in pretend play and

demonstrate an appreciation for dramatic expression.

We are also learning about

Social Studies

Families/Culture

Communities/Civics

History/Time

Geography/Places, People, Environments

Economics

MUSIC & MOVEMENT AREA

Here we are engaged in a variety of musical activities

and demonstrate an appreciation for music.

We are engaged in creative movement

activities and demonstrate an appreciation

for various forms of expressive movement.

We also engage in play and movement to

develop our large motor skills.

COOKING AREA

Here we are engaged in play and interesting

experiences to develop healthy habits.

Assessing Children's Progress Toward Standards

Group Observation Tool

Below is a template of the observation tool that can be used to assess children's progress. Write your own state's standards and benchmarks in the first column. Write children's names across the top. Observe children at play and in their daily activities. This can be done several times a year using different colored ink each time. Collect samples of children's work in portfolios to document their growth. Mark how each child is demonstrating the benchmarks using the following scale:

B   Beginning to Demonstrate

√   Demonstrates Some of the Time

+   Demonstrates Consistently

Beginning of the Year _____   Middle of the Year _____   End of the Year _____

Children's Names

Standard Area: _____ **Standard:** _____ _____ **Benchmarks:**					
1.					
2.					
3.					
4.					
5.					
6.					
7.					
8.					
9.					
10.					

Sample Group Observation Tool for Language and Literacy

B   Beginning to Demonstrate

√   Demonstrates Some of the Time

+   Demonstrates Consistently

Beginning of the Year _____   Middle of the Year _____   End of the Year _____

Children's Names

Standard Area: Language and Literacy **Standard: Reading** **Children use skills and strategies to get meaning from print.** **Benchmarks:**					
1. Demonstrate motivation, interest, and enjoyment in books, reading, and acting out stories while engaged in play					
2. Demonstrate book-handling skills, such as holding a book right-side up and turning pages from front to back					
3. Recognize familiar environmental print, such as "STOP" signs, and realize it has meaning					
4. Retell a story from a familiar book and relate it to real-life experiences					
5. Make predictions of next steps in a story					
6. Demonstrate knowledge that a symbol can represent something else					
7. Recognize own first name in print					
8. Demonstrate knowledge of the *alphabetic principle*, the concept that the sounds of speech can be represented by one or more letters of the alphabet					
9. Identify at least 10 letters of the alphabet, especially those in own name					
10. Demonstrate knowledge of the basic concepts of print, such as knowing the differences between pictures, letters, and words					

Individual Child Observation Tool

Children's individual progress can be kept on a form like the following one. You can begin with a class form and transfer information to an individual form. Write your own state's standards and benchmarks in the first column. Observe children at play and in their daily activities. This can be done several times a year. Collect samples of children's work in portfolios to document their growth. Mark how the child is demonstrating the benchmarks using the following scale:

B   Beginning to Demonstrate

√   Demonstrates Some of the Time

+   Demonstrates Consistently

Child's Name: _____   **Year:** _____

Standard Area: _____	Fall	Winter	Spring
Standard: _____ _____ **Benchmarks:**			
1.			
2.			
3.			
4.			
5.			
6.			
7.			
8.			
9.			
10.			

Sample Individual Child Observation Tool
for Language and Literacy

B   Beginning to Demonstrate

√   Demonstrates Some of the Time

+   Demonstrates Consistently

Child's Name: _____   **Year:** _____

Standard Area: Language and Literacy	Fall	Winter	Spring
Standard: Reading **Children use skills and strategies to get meaning from print.** **Benchmarks:**			
1. Demonstrate motivation, interest, and enjoyment in books, reading, and acting out stories while engaged in play			
2. Demonstrate book-handling skills, such as holding a book right-side up and turning pages from front to back			
3. Recognize familiar environmental print, such as "STOP" signs, and realize it has meaning			
4. Retell a story from a familiar book and relate it to real-life experiences			
5. Makes predictions of next steps in a story			
6. Demonstrate knowledge that a symbol can represent something else			
7. Recognizes own first name in print			
8. Demonstrate knowledge of the *alphabetic principle*, the concept that the sounds of speech can be represented by one or more letters of the alphabet			
9. Identify at least 10 letters of the alphabet, especially those in own name			
10. Demonstrate knowledge of the basic concepts of print, such as knowing the differences between pictures, letters, and words			

Children's Books and Music

Books to Promote Science

Asch, R. (1995). *Water.* San Diego, CA: Harcourt Brace.

Barrett, J. (1970). *Animals should definitely not wear clothing.* New York: Antheneum.

Bernhard, D. (2000). *Earth, sky, wet, dry.* New York: Scholastic.

Blos, J. (1995). *The hungry little boy.* New York: Simon & Schuster Books for Young Readers.

Carle, E. (1969). *The very hungry caterpillar.* New York: Philomel.

Carle, E. (1984). *The very busy spider.* New York: Philomel.

deBourgoing, P. (1989). *Vegetables in the garden.* New York: Scholastic.

dePaola, T. (2002). *Mice squeak, we speak.* East Rutherford, NJ: Penguin Putnam Books for Young Readers.

Ehlert, L. (1988). *Planting a rainbow.* San Diego, CA: Harcourt Brace.

Ehlert, L. (1989). *Color zoo.* New York: HarperCollins.

Ehlert, L. (1990). *Color farm.* New York: Lippincott.

Ehlert, L. (1998). *Nuts to you.* San Diego, CA: Harcourt Brace.

Harris, T. (2000). *Pattern fish.* Brookfield, CT: Millbrook Press.

Hayes, S. (1998). *Eat up, Gemma.* New York: Lothrop, Lee, & Shephard Books.

Hest, A. (1995). *In the rain with baby duck.* Cambridge, MA: Candlewick Press.

Hoban, T. (1971). *Look again.* New York: Macmillan.

Hoban, T. (1981). *Take another look.* New York: Greenwillow Books.

Hoban, T. (1988). *Look, look, look.* New York: Greenwillow Books.

Hoban, J. (1989). *Amy loves the rain.* New York: Harper & Row.

Hoban, J. (1994). *Amy loves the wind.* New York: Scholastic.

Kerley, B. (2002). *A cool drink of water.* Washington DC: National Geographic Society.

Krauss, R. (1945). *The carrot seed.* New York: Scholastic Big Books.

Locker, T. (1997). *Water dance.* San Diego, CA: Harcourt Brace.

London, J. (2001). *Crunch, munch.* San Diego, CA: Silver Whistle/Harcourt.

Nathan, E. (2000). *What do you call a termite home? And other animal homes.* Farmington, MI: Thomson Gale.

Schwartz, D. (1999). *At the pond.* Milwaukee, WI: Gareth Stevens Publishing.

Schwartz, D. (1999). *In a tree.* Milwaukee, WI: Gareth Stevens Publishing.

Stockdale, S. (1997). *Some sleep standing up.* New York: Simon & Schuster Books for Young Readers.

Tuxworth, N. (1999). *Animal homes.* Milwaukee: Gareth Stevens Pub.

Waddell, M. (1992). *Owl babies.* Cambridge, MA: Candlewick Press.

Books to Promote Social Studies and Multicultural Understanding

Brown, E. (1994). *Handa's surprise.* New York: Scholastic.

Daly, N. (1999). *Jamela's dress.* New York: Farrar, Straus & Giroux.

Fleming, C. (2004). *This is the baby.* New York: Melanie Kroupa Books.

Fox, M. (1989). *Shoes from grandpa.* New York: Orchard Books.

Hamanaka, S. (1994). *All the colors of the earth.* New York: Harper Trophy.

Hutchins, P. (1983). *You'll soon grow into them, Titch.* New York: Greenwillow Books.

Intrater, R. (2000). *Two eyes, a nose, and a mouth.* New York: Scholastic.

Kates, B. (1992). *We're different, we're the same.* New York: Random House.

Katz, K. (1999). *The color of us.* New York: Scholastic.

Klamath County YMCA Family Preschool. (1993). *The land of many colors.* New York: Scholastic.

Morris, A. (1993). *Bread, bread, bread.* New York: Mulberry Books.

Pellegrini, N. (1991). *Families are different.* New York: Scholastic.

Smith, C. (2000). *Jingle dancer.* New York: HarperCollins.

Taback, S. (1999). *Joseph had a little overcoat.* New York: Viking.

Watanabe, S. (1979). *How do I put it on?* New York: HarperCollins.

Wells, R. (1991). *Max's dragon shirt.* New York: Penguin Books.

Wells, R. (1998). *Yoko.* New York: Hyperion Books for Children.

Books to Promote Language and Literacy

Bang, M. (1983). *Ten, nine, eight.* New York: Greenwillow Books.

Brett, J. (1989). *The mitten.* New York: Putnam & Grosset.

Carle, E. (1997). *From head to toe.* New York: HarperCollins.

Carle, E. (2001). *Today is Monday.* New York: Philomel Books.

Ehlert, L. (1996). *Eating the alphabet.* San Diego, CA: Hartcourt Brace.

Fleming, D. (1991). *In the tall, tall grass.* New York: Henry Holt.

Fleming, D. (1992). *Lunch.* New York: Henry Holt.

Fleming, D. (1993). *In the small, small pond.* New York: Henry Holt.

Guarino, D. (1989). *Is your mama a llama?* New York: Scholastic.

Hill, E. (1997). *Spot goes to the farm.* East Rutherford, NJ: Penguin Putnam Books for Young Readers.

Kubler, A. (2005). *Sign and sing along: Twinkle, twinkle little star.* Wiltshire, UK: Child's Play International.

Martin, B., & Carle, E. (1983). *Brown bear, brown bear, what do you see?* New York: Henry Holt.

McCloskey, R. (1948). *Blueberries for Sal.* New York: Pantheon.

Raffi. (1990). *The wheels on the bus (Raffi songs to read).* New York: Crown Books for Young Readers.

Seuss, D. (1957). *Cat in the hat.* Boston: Houghton Mifflin.

Shaw, C. (1988). *It looked like spilt milk.* New York: Harper.

Books to Promote Learning New Languages

Beinstein, P. (2002). *Dora's book of words [Libro de palabras de dora].* New York: Scholastic.

Brown, M. W. (1957). *Good night moon.* New York: Harper & Row.

Brown, M. W. (1995). *Buenas noches luna.* New York: HarperCollins.

Emberley, R. (1993). *My day/Mi dia.* Boston: Little, Brown.

Emberley, R. (2000). *My opposites/Mis opuestos.* Boston: Little, Brown.

Emberley, R. (2000). *My shapes/Mis formas.* Boston: Little Brown.

Mora, P. (1996). *Uno, dos, tres: One, two, three.* New York: Clarion Books.

Orozoco, J. L. (1997). *Diez deditos/Ten little fingers, and other play rhymes and action songs from Latin America.* New York: Dutton Children's Books.

Sendak, M. (1963). *Where the wild things are.* New York: HarperCollins.

Sendak, M. (1996). *Donde viven los monstruos.* New York: HarperCollins.

Books to Promote Mathematics

Anno, M. (1982). *Anno's counting book.* New York: Philomel.

Burris, P. (2003). *Five green and speckled frogs.* New York: Scholastic.

Carle, E. (1968). *One, two, three to the zoo: A counting book.* New York: Scholastic.

Christelow, E. (1989). *Five little monkeys jumping on the bed.* New York: Clarion Books.

Ehlert, L. (1990). *Fish eyes: A book you can count on.* New York: Harcourt.

Fleming, D. (1992). *Count.* New York: Henry Holt.

Foglesong G. (1996). *Fiesta!* New York: Greenwillow Books.

Gillen, P. B. (1988). *My signing book of numbers.* Washington, DC: Kendall Green.

Hoban, T. (1972). *Count and see.* New York: Macmillan.
Hoban, T. (1985). *Is it larger? Is it smaller?* New York: Greenwillow Books.
Hoban, T. (1985). *1, 2, 3.* New York: Greenwillow Books.
Hoban, T. (1986). *Shapes, shapes, shapes.* New York: Greenwillow Books.
Hoban, T. (1998). *More, fewer, less.* New York: Greenwillow Books.
Hoban, T. (1999). *Let's count.* New York: Greenwillow Books.
Lionni, L. (1960). *Inch by inch.* New York: Harper Children's.
Mallett, D. (1995). *Inch by inch: The garden song.* New York: HarperCollins.
Paparone, P. (1995). *Five little ducks.* New York: Scholastic (Big Book).
Peek, M. (1981). *Roll over.* New York: Clarion Books.
Pinkney, B. (1994). *Max found two sticks.* New York: Simon & Schuster.
Stobbs, W. (1984). *1, 2 buckle my shoe.* Oxford, UK: Oxford University Press.

Books to Promote Social–Emotional Development

Bourgeois, P., & Clark B. (1995). *Franklin wants a pet.* New York: Scholastic.
Bourgeois, P., & Clark B. (2000). *Franklin helps out.* New York: Scholastic.
Freymann, S., & Elffers, J. (1999). *How are you peeling? Foods with moods.* New York: Scholastic.
Isadora, R. (2000). *Friends.* New York: Greenwillow Books.
Lionni, L. (1963). *Swimmy.* New York: Pantheon.
Lionni, L. (1985). *It's mine.* New York: Scholastic.
Rogers, F. (1996). *Making friends.* New York: Putnam Juvenile.

Books to Support a Successful Transition to Kindergarten

Penn, A. (1993). *The kissing hand.* New York: Scholastic.
Rockwell, A. (2001). *Welcome to kindergarten.* New York: Scholastic.
Senisi, E. (1994). *Kindergarten kids.* New York: Scholastic.
Slate, J. (1996). *Miss Bindergarten gets ready for kindergarten.* New York: Scholastic.
Wild, M., & Legge, D. (1999). *Tom goes to kindergarten.* New York: Scholastic.
Wing, N. (2001). *The night before kindergarten.* New York: Scholastic.

Children's Music

Jenkins, E. (2003). Day-O. *Sharing cultures with Ella Jenkins* [CD]. Washington, DC: Smithsonian Folkways Recordings.
Raffi. (1998). Wiloughby Wallaby Woo. *Singable songs for the very young: Great with a peanut-butter sandwich* [CD]. Cambridge, MA: Rounder/Umgd.

Resources for Teaching Bilingual Learners

American Library Association:
http://www.alastore.ala.org

Bess Press:
http://www.besspress.com

Bilingual References:
http://www.sasked.gov.sk.ca/docs/indlang/langcu11.html

China Sprout:
www.chinasprout.com

Libros Sin Fronteras:
http://www.librossinfronteras.com

Principles of Bilingual Education:
http://coe.sdsu.edu/people/jmora/TheoryBEMMdl/

Project CLAS:
http://clas.uiuc.edu/index.html

Reading and English Language Learners, by Beth Antunez:
http://www.readingrockets.org/article.php?ID=409

Research on Bilingual Reading Instruction:
http://www.ncela.gwu.edu/pathways/reading/

Shen's Books:
http://www.shens.com

Teaching Children Spanish, French, and German:
http://www.literacycenter.net/lessonview_es.htm#

Teaching Indigenous Languages:
http://jan.ucc.nau.edu/~jar/TIL.html

Assessment Materials

The Creative Curriculum Developmental Continuum Assessment System, developed by Diane Trister Dodge, Laura Colker, and Cate Heroman:
Available from http://www.teachingstrategies.com

Early Childhood Environment Rating Scale (ECERS), revised edition, developed by Thelma Harmes, Richard Clifford, and Debby Cryer:
Available from http://www.teacherscollegepress.com

Early Language and Literacy Classroom Observation (ELLCO) Toolkit, developed by Miriam Smith and David Dickinson, with Angela Sangeore and Louisa Anastasopoulos
Available from http://www.brookespublishing.com

The Preschool Child Observation Record, developed by High/Scope:
Available from http://www.highscope.org

The Work Sampling System, developed by Samuel Miesels:
Available from http://www.pearsonearlylearning.com

Helpful Web Sites

Center on the Social and Emotional Foundations for Early Learning:
http://www.csefel.uiuc.edu

Children's Technology Review, ratings for children's software and Web sites:
http://www.childrenssoftware.com

Early Childhood Education Assessment Consortium, Council of Chief State School Officers
Information on early learning standards and links to state standards:
http://www.ccsso.org/ECEAstandards

National Association for the Education of Young Children (NAEYC):
http://www.naeyc.org

National Childcare Information Center Web Site
The Gray Center for Social Learning and Understanding has resources on social stories:
http://www.thegraycenter.org

Links to every state's early learning guidelines:
http://www.nccic.org/pubs/goodstart/elgwebsites.html

References

Althouse, R., Johnson, M., & Mitchel, S. (2003). *The colors of learning: Integrating the visual arts into the early childhood curriculum.* New York: Teachers College Press.

Baker, A. C., & Manfredi/Petitt, L. A. (2004). *Relationships, the heart of quality care.* Washington, DC: National Association for the Education of Young Children.

Berk, L., & Winsler, A. (1995). *Scaffolding children's learning: Vygotsky and early childhood education.* Washington, DC: National Association for the Education of Young Children.

Bodrova, E., & Leong, D. (1996). *Tools of the mind.* Columbus, OH: Prentice Hall.

Bodrova, E., Leong, D., Paynter, D., & Semenov, D. (2000). *A framework for early literacy instruction: Aligning standards to developmental patterns and student behaviors, pre-K through kindergarten.* Aurora, CO: Mid-Continent Research for Education and Learning.

Bowman, B. T., Donovan, M. S., & Burns, M. S. (Eds.). (2000). *Eager to learn: Educating our preschoolers.* Washington, DC: National Academies Press. Available online at http://www.nap.edu

Bredekamp, S., & Copple, C. (1997). *Developmentally appropriate practice in early childhood programs* (Rev. ed.). Washington, DC: National Association for the Education of Young Children. Position statement available online at www.naeyc.org/about/positions/pdf/PSDAP98.pdf

Bruner, J. S. (1972). The nature and uses of immaturity. *American Psychologist, 27,* 687–708.

Burns, M. S., Griffin, P., & Snow, C. (1999). *Starting out right: A guide to promoting children's reading success.* Washington, DC: National Academies Press.

Carson, R. (1965). *The sense of wonder.* New York: Harper & Row.

Chalufour, I., & Worth, K. (2003). *Discovering nature with young children.* St. Paul, MN: Redleaf Press.

Chard, S. (1998). *The project approach: Making curriculum come alive.* New York: Scholastic.

Chenfeld, M. (1993). *Teaching in the key of life.* Washington, DC: National Association for the Education of Young Children.

Chrisman, K. (2005). The nuts and bolts of discovery centers. *Science and Young Children, 43*(3), 20–23.

Clements, D. (1999). The effective use of computers with young children. In J. V. Copley (Ed.), *Mathematics in the early years* (pp. 119–128). Reston, VA: National Council of Teachers of Mathematics.

Colker, L. (2002). Teaching and learning about science. *Young Children, 57*(5), 10–11, 47.

Copple, C., & Bredekamp, S. (2006). *Basics of developmentally appropriate practice.* Washington, DC: National Association for the Education of Young Children.

Council on Physical Education for Children of the National Association for Sport and Physical Education. (2000). *Appropriate practices in movement programs for young children ages 3–5.* Reston, VA: Council on Physical Education for Children of the National Association for Sport and Physical Education.

Curtis, D., & Carter, M. (2003). *Designs for living and learning: Transforming early childhood environments.* St. Paul, MN: Redleaf Press.

D'Addesio, J., Grob, B., Furman, L., Hayes, K., & David, J. (2005). Learning about the world around us. *Young Children, 60*(5), 50–57.

Derman-Sparks, L. (1989). *Anti-biased curriculum: Tools for empowering young children.* Washington, DC: National Association for the Education of Young Children.

Dodge, D., Colker, L., & Heroman, C. (2002). *The creative curriculum for preschool* (4th ed.). Washington, DC: Teaching Strategies.

Edwards, C., Forman, G., & Gandini, L. (Eds.). (1998). *The hundred languages of children.* Westport, CT: Greenwood Press.

Haugland, S., & Wright, J. (1997). *Young children and technology: A world of discovery.* Boston: Allyn & Bacon.

Helm, J., & Beneke, S., & Steinheimer, K. (1998). *Windows on learning: Documenting young children's work.* New York: Teachers College Press.

Hyson, M. (2004). *The emotional development of young children: Building an emotion-centered curriculum.* New York: Teachers College Press.

Hyson, M. (in press). *Enthusiastic and engaged: Strengthening young children's positive approaches to learning.* New York: Teachers College Press.

International Reading Association & the National Association for the Education of Young Children. (1998). *Learning to read and write: Developmentally appropriate practices for young children* (Joint position statement). Washington, DC: National Association for the Education of Young Children. Available online at http://www.naeyc.org/about/positions/pdf/PSREAD98.pdf

Katz, L., & Chard, S. (2000). *Engaging children's minds: The project approach* (2nd ed.). Westport, CT: Greenwood Press.

Lasky, L., & Mukerji-Bergeson, R. (1980). *Art: Basic for young children.* Washington, DC: National Association for the Education of Young Children.

McAfee, O., Leong, D., & Bodrova, E. (2004). *Basics of assessment: A primer for early childhood educators.* Washington, DC: National Association for the Education of Young Children.

Meier, D. (2004). *The young child's memory for words: Developing first and second language and literacy.* New York: Teachers College Press.

Mindes, G. (2005). Social studies in today's early childhood curricula. *Young Children, 60*(5), 12–18.

Mitchell, A., & David, J. (Eds.). (1992). *Explorations with young children: A curriculum guide from the Bank Street College of Education.* Beltsville, MD: Gryphon House; Reston, VA: National Association for Sport and Physical Education.

National Association for the Education of Young Children. (1995). *Responding to linguistic and cultural diversity: Recommendations for effective early childhood education* (Position statement). Washington, DC: Author. Available online at www.naeyc.org/about/positions/PSDIV98.asp

National Association for the Education of Young Children. (1996). *Technology and young children: Ages 3 through 8* (Position statement). Washington, DC: Author. Available online at http://naeyc.org/about/positions/PSTECH98.pdf

National Association for the Education of Young Children. (2005). *NAEYC early childhood program standards and accreditation criteria: The mark of quality in early childhood education.* Washington, DC: Author. Available online at www.naeyc.org/accreditation/next_era.asp

National Association for the Education of Young Children & the National Association of Early Childhood Specialists in State Departments of Education. (2002). *Early learning standards: Creating the conditions for success.* Washington, DC: Author. Available online at http://naeyc.org/about/positions/learning_standards.asp

National Association for Sport and Physical Education. (2002). *Active start: A statement of physical activity guidelines for children birth to five years.* Reston, VA: National Association for Sport and Physical Education.

National Council for the Social Studies. (1993, January/February). Definition approved. *Social Studies Professional, 114,* p. 3.

National Council of Teachers of Mathematics and the National Association for the Education of Young Children. (2002). *Early childhood mathematics: Promoting good beginnings* (Position statement). Washington, DC: National Association for the Education of Young Children. Available online at http://naeyc.org/about/positions/mathematics.asp

Neuman, S. B., Copple, C., & Bredekamp, S. (2000). *Learning to read and write: Developmentally appropriate practices for young children.* Washington, DC: National Association for the Education of Young Children.

Neuman, S. B., & Dickinson, D. (Eds.). (2001). *The handbook of early literacy research.* New York: Guildford.

Piaget, J. (1952). *The origins of intelligence in children.* New York: International University Press.

Pianta, R. (2002). *School readiness: A focus on children, families, communities, and schools.* Arlington, VA: Educational Research Service.

Pianta, R., & Kraft-Sayre, M. (2003). *Successful kindergarten transition: Your guide to connecting children, families, and schools.* Baltimore, MD: Brookes.

Pianta, R., & Walsh, D. (1996). *High-risk children in schools: Creating sustaining relationships.* New York: Routledge.

Sanders, S. (2002). *Active for life: Developmentally appropriate movement programs for young children.* Washington, DC: National Association for the Education of Young Children.

Saracho, O., & Spodek, B. (2003). Recent trends and innovations in the early childhood education curriculum. *Early Child Development and Care 173*(2–3), 175–183.

Seefeldt, C. (2001). *Social studies for the preschool/primary child.* Upper Saddle River, NJ: Merrill, Prentice Hall.

Shalaway, L. (2005). *Learning to teach: Not just for beginners.* New York: Scholastic.

Shonkoff, J. P., & Phillips, D. A. (Eds.). (2000). *From neurons to neighborhoods: The science of early childhood development.* Committee on Integrating the Science of Early Childhood Development, Board on Children, Youth, and Families, National Research Council and Institute of Medicine: Washington, DC: National Academy Press. Available at http://www.nap.edu

Shore, R. (1997). *Rethinking the brain: New insights into early development.* New York: Families and Work Institute.

Sipe, L. R. (2001). Invention, convention, and intervention: Invented spelling and the teacher's role. *Reading Teacher, 55*(3), 264–273.

Snow, C., Burns, M. S., & Griffin, P. (Eds.). (1998). *Preventing reading difficulties in young children.* Washington, DC: National Academies Press.

Sulzby, E. (1985). Children's emergent reading of favorite storybooks. *Reading Research Quarterly, 20*, 458–481.

Vukelich, C., Christie, J., & Enz, B. (2002). *Helping young children learn language and literacy.* Boston: Allyn & Bacon.

Vygotsky, L. S. (1978). *Mind in society: The development of higher mental processes* (M. Cole, V. John-Steiner, S. Scribner, & E. Souberman, Eds. & Trans.). Cambridge, MA: Harvard University Press.

Worth, K., & Grollman, S. (2003). *Worms, shadows, and whirlpools: Science in the early childhood classroom.* Portsmouth, NH: Heinemann.

Wurm, J. (2005). *Working in the Reggio way: A beginner's guide for American teachers.* St. Paul, MN: Redleaf Press.

For Further Reading

Bodrova, E., Leong, D. J., Paynter, D. E., & Hensen, R. (2003). *Scaffolding literacy development in the preschool classroom* (Rev. ed.). Aurora, CO: Mid-Continent Research for Education and Learning.

Chalufour, I., & Worth, K. (2004). *Building structures with young children.* St. Paul, MN: Redleaf Press and the National Association for the Education of Young Children.

Chalufour, I., & Worth, K. (2005). *Exploring water with young children.* St. Paul, MN: Redleaf Press and the National Association for the Education of Young Children.

Clements, D., & Sarama, J. (Eds.). 2004. *Engaging young children in mathematics.* Mahwah, NJ: Lawrence Erlbaum.

Copley, J. (Ed.). (1999). *Mathematics in the early years.* Washington, DC: National Association for the Education of Young Children and National Council of Teachers of Mathematics.

Copple, C. (Ed.). (2003). *A world of difference: Readings on teaching young children in a diverse society.* Washington, DC: National Association for the Education of Young Children.

Dragan, P. (2005). *Teaching English language learners.* Portsmouth, NH: Heinemann.

Dodge, D., Heroman, C., Charles, J., & Maiorca, J. (2004). Beyond outcomes: How ongoing assessment supports children's learning and leads to meaningful curriculum. *Young Children, 59*(1), 20–28.

Gartrell, D. (2004). *The power of guidance: Teaching social emotional skills in early childhood classrooms.* Clifton Park: NY: Thompson Delmar Learning; Washington, DC: National Association for the Education of Young Children.

Gronlund, G. (2006). *Making early learning standards come alive: Connecting your practice and curriculum to state guidelines.* St. Paul, MN: Redleaf Press and the National Association for the Education of Young Children.

Helm, J., & Beneke, S. (Eds.). (2003). *The power of projects: Meeting contemporary challenges in early childhood classrooms.* New York: Teachers College Press.

Helm, J., & Katz, L. (2000). *Young investigators: The project approach in the early years.* New York: Teachers College Press.

Kaiser, B., & Rasminsky, J. (2002). *Challenging behavior in young children: Understanding, preventing, and responding effectively.* Boston: Allyn & Bacon.

Morrow, L. M. (2001). *Literacy development in the early years.* Boston: Allyn & Bacon.

Odom, L. L., Wolery, R., Lieber, J., & Horn, E. (2002). *Widening the circle: Including children with disabilities in preschool programs.* New York: Teachers College Press.

Sandall, S., McLean, M., & Smith, B. (2000). *DEC recommended practices in early intervention/early childhood special education.* Denver, CO: Division of Early Childhood of the Council for Exceptional Children.

Schickendanz, J. A., & Casbergue, R. M. (2004). *Writing in preschool: Learning to orchestrate meaning and marks.* Newark, DE: International Reading Association.

Seefelt, C. (2005). *How to work with standards in the early childhood classroom.* New York: Teachers College Press.

Shiller, P. (1999). *Start smart! Building brain power in the early years.* Beltsville, MD: Gryphon House.

Tabors, P. (1997). *One child, two languages: A guide for preschool educators of children learning English as a second language.* Baltimore, MD: Brookes.

Trepanier-Street, M. (2000). Multiple forms of representation in long-term projects: The garden project. *Childhood Education, 77*(1), 18–24.

Zigler, E., Singer, D., & Bishop-Josef, S. (2004). *Children's play: The roots of reading.* Washington, DC: Zero to Three.

Index

Algebra, 90, 97–98
American Council for the Arts in Education, 101–102
American Red Cross, 127
Appreciation, 27, 35–36
Approaches to learning, 25–32
Art, 101–114
Art area, 20, 28, 76, 104, 122, 141
Assessment tools:
    documentation, 9–10
    observation tools, 9, 144–147
    resources, 151

Baker, A., 14
Banana Pudding recipe, 126
Bank Street College of Education, 58
Benchmarks, 2
    See also Assessment tools
Bilingual learners:
    creative arts, 113
    health and physical development, 127
    individual developmental needs, 3
    literacy skills, 85–86
    mathematics skills, 98–99
    approaches to learning, 25–32
    resources, 150–151
    science skills, 54–55
    social studies skills, 66
Block area, 28, 75
Bookmaking, 78
Book resources, 148–150
Brainstorming:
    See Problem-solving skills
Bruner, J. S., 5
Bubble recipe, 47–48
Burns, M. S., 69
Butter recipe, 65

Carson, R., 41, 131
Chenfeld, M. B., 14
Child-friendly environments:
    basic concepts, 13–23
    creative arts, 104
    health and physical development, 119–122
    individual developmental needs, 38
    literacy areas, 71–73

    mathematics, 92
    science/discovery areas, 43–44
    social-emotional development, 28–29
    social studies, 59–60
Civics, 58, 62–63
Classroom environments:
    See Child-friendly environments
Clay and play dough, 107–108, 125
Collages, 108
Communication skills, 70, 80–82
Community spirit, 14–15, 35–37, 58, 62–63
Computer area, 19, 76
Computer skills, 52, 53
Consortium of National Arts Education Associations, 102
Cooking area, 143
Cooperation, 27, 36–37
Council on Physical Education for Children, 117
Creative arts, 101–114
Creative Curriculum Developmental Continuum Assessment System, 9
Creative movement, 102, 110–112
Cultural awareness, 58, 60–62
Curiosity, 26, 29
Curriculum design, 3–8, 131–136

Daily schedules, 21–22
Dance, 111–112
Data analysis, 90, 96–97
Derman-Sparks, L., 84
Developmentally appropriate practice (DAP), 3
Dickinson, D., 69
Discovery/Science area, 19, 43–44, 141
Diversity, 26, 35–36
Dramatic play, 102, 112–113
Dramatic play area, 19, 29, 65–66, 75, 105, 122, 142
Dress-up clothes, 19

Eagerness, 26, 29
Early learning guidelines:
    creative arts, 102
    health and physical development, 118
    approaches to learning, 25–32

literacy skills, 70
mathematics skills, 90
preschool, 2
science skills, 42
social-emotional development, 27
social studies, 58
web sites, 151–152
See also Preschool content standards
Earth science, 42, 51–52
Eating habits, 125–127
Economics, 58, 65–66
Emberley, R., 66
Emotion regulation, 26–28, 34–35
Environment and science, 42, 53–54
Exercise, 117–129

Family relationships, 15–16, 58, 60–62, 86
Filipino Pancit recipe, 128
Fine motor skills, 118, 124–125
Flexibility, 21
Focused studies, 43, 58–59, 91, 132–136
Foreign language skills, 70, 82–85
Friendships, 35–37

Gardens, 49–50, 127
Geography, 58, 63–65
Geometry and shapes, 90, 94–95
Good Start, Grow Smart, 2
Griffin, P., 69
Gross motor skills, 118, 122–124

Hands-on experiences:
    developmentally appropriate practice (DAP), 3
    economics, 65
    importance, 18
    learning approaches, 4
    literacy skills, 72–73, 81
    mathematics skills, 89–90, 92–99
    scheduling flexibility, 21
    science skills, 41–42, 44–54
    social studies, 57
Healthy lifestyles, 117–129
History, 58, 63
Hyson, M., 26, 28

Imagination, 26, 32
Individual developmental needs:
    creative arts, 113–114
    health and physical development, 128
    literacy skills, 86–87
    mathematics skills, 99
    positive approaches, 3, 38–39
    science skills, 55
    social studies skills, 66–67
Initiative, 26, 30–31
Interest areas, 16–21, 28–29, 139–143
Invention, 26, 32

Kindergarten transition, 136–137
Kraft-Sayre, M., 136

Language skills, 70, 82–85
Learning approaches:
    interest areas, 16–21
    play, 4–5, 21
    See also Project Approach
Library area, 7, 28, 71–72
Life science, 42, 49–50
Listening area, 140
Listening skills, 70, 79–80
Literacy skills, 69–87
Long-term projects:
    See Focused studies; Project Approach

Manfredi/Petitt, L., 14
Manners, 36, 37
Math area, 19, 76, 140
Mathematics skills, 89–99
Measurement skills, 90, 95–96
Modeling:
    computer skills, 53
    creative arts, 109
    emotions, 34–35
    good manners, 37
    health and physical development, 118, 128
    language use, 86
    mathematics skills, 98
    problem-solving skills, 31
    writing skills, 77
Montessori, Maria, 13
Movement, 102, 110–112, 117–122
Music, 102, 109–110, 150
Music and movement area, 20,
    104, 122, 143

National Association for Sport and Physical
    Education (NASPE), 117–118
National Association for the Education of
    Young Children (NAEYC), 15, 73, 89, 131, 152
National Association of Early Childhood Specialists
    in State Departments of Education, 131
National Childcare Information Center, 2, 152
National Council for the Social Studies
    (NCSS), 57, 58
National Council of Teachers of Mathematics
    (NCTM), 89–90, 99
National Research Council, 41, 69
National Science Education Standards, 42
Neighborhood environment, 63–65
Neuman, S. B., 17, 69
New languages, 70, 82–85
Number sense and operations,
    90, 92–97

Observation tools, 9, 144–147
Oral language development, 70, 80–82

Painting and drawing, 105–106
Pancit recipe, 128
Papermaking, 54

Parent involvement, 15–16, 118, 136
Passage of time, 58, 63
Pattern identification skills, 90, 97–98
Persistence, 26, 30–31
Personal health habits, 118, 125–127
Pets, 7–8
Phonological awareness, 69, 79, 80
Physical development, 117–129
Physical science, 42, 46–49
Piaget, J., 5
Pianta, R., 136, 137–138
Planning guidelines, 133
Play, 4–5, 21, 25
Play Dough recipe, 107
Portfolios, 9
Preschool Child Observation Record, 9
Preschool content standards:
    characteristics, 1–2
    creative arts, 102, 105–113
    curriculum design, 3–8, 131–136
    health and physical development, 118, 122–127
    individual developmental needs, 3, 38–39, 55, 66–67, 86–87
    approaches to learning, 25–32
    literacy skills, 70–72, 73–85
    mathematics skills, 89–90, 92–98
    science skills, 41–42, 44–54
    social-emotional development, 27–28, 33–37
    social studies, 58, 60–66
Pretzels in a Bag, 96
Printmaking, 107
Probability, 90, 96–97
Problem-solving skills, 26, 31–32
    See also Mathematics skills; Science explorations
Project Approach:
    basic concepts, 5–8
    creative arts, 103
    documentation, 10
    health and physical development, 119
    learning approaches, 27–28
    literacy skills, 70–71
    mathematics skills, 91
    science, 43
    social studies, 58–59
    topic exploration, 132–136
Prop Boxes, 112
Pro-social behaviors, 26, 36–37

Reading area, 18, 71–72, 139
Reading skills, 69–70, 73–75
Recycling, 54
Reflection, 26, 31–32
Reggio Emilia, Italy, 5, 16, 103
Relationship-building, 13–16, 35–37
Relaxation skills, 35

Resources, 139–152
Respect, 14, 27, 35–36, 53–54
Role-play scenarios, 35

Safe practices, 118, 125–127
Schedules, 21–22
Science area, 19, 28, 43–44, 76, 141
Science explorations, 41–55
Scientific inquiry, 42, 45–46
Self-concept, 27, 33–34
Self-confidence, 27, 33–34
Shared writing, 77
Similarities and differences
    See Diversity
Snacks and food, 126
Snow, C., 69
Social-emotional development, 25–28, 33–37
Social studies, 57–67
Space science, 42, 51–52
Speaking skills, 70, 80–82
Standards:
    See Preschool content standards
Sulzby, E., 76
Synapses, 18

Table toys, 122
Technology and science, 42, 52–53
Topic exploration, 5–8, 132–136
Transition to Kindergarten, 136–137

Visual arts, 102, 105–109
Vygotsky, L. S., 5, 9, 81

Walsh, D., 137–138
Water and sand area, 20
Web sites, 150–152
Welcoming environments:
    basic concepts, 13–23
    creative arts, 104
    health and physical development, 119–122
    individual developmental needs, 38
    literacy areas, 71–72
    mathematics, 92
    science/discovery areas, 43–44
    social-emotional development, 28–29
    social studies, 59–60
Woodworking, 108
Work Sampling System, 9
Writing area, 18, 72, 75, 122, 139
Writing skills, 69–70, 75–78

Zone of proximal development, 5

Corwin Press

The Corwin Press logo—a raven striding across an open book—represents the union of courage and learning. Corwin Press is committed to improving education for all learners by publishing books and other professional development resources for those serving the field of PreK–12 education. By providing practical, hands-on materials, Corwin Press continues to carry out the promise of its motto: **"Helping Educators Do Their Work Better."**